Winning Husband

Jessica Lowe

Copyright © 2024 by Jessica Lowe

All rights reserved.

No portion of this book may be reproduced in any form without written permission from the publisher or author, except as permitted by U.S. copyright law.

Contents

1. Part 1 — 1
2. Part 2 — 5
3. Part 3 — 11
4. Part 4 — 15
5. Part 5 — 20
6. Part 6 — 25
7. Part 7 — 30
8. Part 8 — 35
9. Part 9 — 40
10. Part 10 — 44
11. Part 11 — 48
12. Part 12 — 54
13. Part 13 — 59
14. Part 14 — 66
15. Part 15 — 73

16.	Part 16	77
17.	Part 17	85
18.	Part 18	91
19.	Part 19	98
20.	Part 20	105
21.	Part 21	110
22.	Part 22	115
23.	Part 23	121
24.	Part 24	125
25.	Part 25	130
26.	Part 26	134
27.	Part 27	138
28.	Part 28	142
29.	Part 29	148
30.	Part 30	155
31.	Part 31	159
32.	Part 32	165
33.	Part 33	169
34.	Part 34	173
35.	Part 35	178
36.	Part 36	182
37.	Part 37	188
38.	Part 38	193

39. Part 39   198

40. Part 40   202

41. Epilogue   209

Part 1

The palanquin came to a stop in front of a familiar house that we come to quite frequently. I slowly stepped out making sure to fix my dress to get rid of any wrinkles that might have formed.

"Make sure to control your facial expressions once we go inside, do you hear me?" I glanced over at my mother once those words left her lips. She gave me a stern look and I bowed my head down in embarrassment recalling the last time I made a ruckus when we went to Lady Byeol's residence for tea.

"But she started it mother, pushing her son's marriage into every topic that we talked about together. How am I supposed to answer to such obvious suggestions?" When we got invited for tea last time, I patiently listened to that woman's blabbering for a few hours until I couldn't handle it anymore. I calmly told her that her son wasn't exactly to my liking so she got mad and tried to pick a fight with me, insulting me about being ungrateful.

Mother fixed a loose strand of my hair into place before sighing. "But Goeun-ah, there was no reason to start talking back to her like that. Those women in there will spread horrible rumors about you if you keep acting up like that. Do you want your mother's reputation to go down by people saying that I didn't raise my daughter right?" Mother was pretty sensitive when it came to these things and would always be strict with me.

I shook my head no before opening the door to go inside. Manners and etiquette was a big thing here for nobles and one small mistake could result in your whole family's honor tumbling down. From a young age, I was to take lessons to learn how to walk, talk, and even breathe gracefully. I would have to learn embroidery, painting, and calligraphy. My childhood passed by like that, with hours of practicing to master all the things that society put as a must for us women to know.

"Greetings Lady Byeol and Lady Kang, thank you for inviting us over today. It's a pleasure to be here."

"I hope you weren't offended by my actions last time Lady Byeol"

"No no, the pleasure is mine, come in come in. The tea will get cold and all the ladies are waiting inside." They ushered us in and I quickly looked around for anyone that I knew to spend the remaining of my time here with.

Once we arrived back at home, I greeted my father briefly before going into my room. My room was redesigned a few days ago due to the constant requests I made to father saying how my preferences changed as a I grew older.

I sat down and my maids came in to help take off all the accessories off of my hair. "Would you like us to prepare a bath for you my lady?" "a hot bath will soothe your muscles and help you to relax.."

"Father asked for my presense in his study room after this, so just help me with my hair for today Areum-ah." She quickly got to work and started to brush my hair, making me feel a little sleepy. "If it wasn't for you, I don't think I would ever be able to take care of all this long hair myself"

"Well that is my job my lady." Areum chuckled and a smile went on my face.

"Father, you called for me?" I made my way to where he was sitting and took a seat across from him. Father was around the age of 40s and was starting to get white hair around his head and beard. He glanced up from the papers he was looking over before putting it down.

"Goeun-ah, I had something to tell you today since it's a matter regarding you, the only daughter of the Han family." "And you are turning 19 this year, a very suitable age" He passed a letter to me and I hesitantly took it before reading the contents.

We request that all families with eligible girls submit their names to participate in the Selection of the Crown princess. They are to be tested and then chosen to become the spouse for Crown Prince Jong Yul.

I looked up at father with wide eyes and then pointed between me and the letter.

Father cleared his throat a little uncomfortably. "Since it's a royal edict, we can't reject and there's no need to when an opportunity like this has arisen. Becoming family with the royal family is a once in a lifetime opportunity my child."

I gaped my mouth open and shut not knowing what to say for a bit. So my opinion is once again thrown out the window somewhere. I straightened up my posture and cleared my throat a little uncomfortably. "when will I be leaving for the palace then?"

Father brightened up at my words and wore a big smile on his face. "In a few days so I want you to start packing and getting yourself ready. Your mother has already started to pack the stuff you will take when she heard about it."

I played with the corner of my dress out of nervousness and a little bit of annoyance.

"oh" was all I could say since they already seemed to be ready to wave me off goodbye and all they needed to do was deliver the news. Even if I had refused, I would've still been on that palanquin traveling to the palace in a few days, whether I liked it or not.

Part 2

"Make sure to follow what they say and not cause any trouble there." "Always wear a smile on your face and treat everyone with respect, especially the crown prince" Mother kept drilling all these things into my head since the crack of dawn and I know I was forming a headache.

"You better not skip your meals, it's an order" I whipped my head around with a warm smile. Finally, someone said something that made me feel happy . I looked up to see my big brother standing on the sideline next to father pretending not to care about me leaving.

"Atleast come home once or twice a month brother. It's sad to see you coming home just to see me off" With a pout I got into the planquinn and bid all of them goodbye.

It was a smooth ride and I took a quick nap to shake off the headache I was feeling. I woke up once I heard a thud from outside. The gates to the palace had opened and I slowly got off and stretched my slightly numb legs.

I tried to keep my gaze down but the curiosity in me overtook that and I silently looked at my surroundings. Yeah, no one should doubt the wealth of the royal family

The scenery was amazing and the buildings were like an artwork, to say the least. I quietly reminded myself to close my mouth before flies went in. I am a noble but them..they are on a whole another level.

I composed myself as a lady wearing a green dress came over to my side with a few ladies behind her.

"Lady Han Goeun, I am to be escorting you to your chambers and help you with your stay here in the palace. I am Court Lady Choi, the one in charge of running the crown princess selection."

I quickly bowed down to show my respect. "ah- yes. I hope you take good care of me Court lady Choi."

As I walked behind her, I took note of the directions she was taking and all the places she was introducing me to. A mini tour around the palace. I doubt I will remember any of that but I tried hard to follow along with her.

"This is where you'll be staying. If you need any help whatsoever, we left 2 maids to be helping every lady here." "we will all be meeting for breakfast tomorrow once all the ladies arrive." She looked over my shoulder and I turned around to see what she was looking at.

I got a jumpscare seeing 2 girls behind me bowing their heads down. I didn't even realize how stealthy they can be. When did they arrive?

"Thank you for such a generous welcome, I hope we all get along well" With that being said, I went inside my now new room and got changed into a more comfortable gown before heading out for dinner again.

The sun was slowly setting, casting an orangish pink look all over the palace buildings. Once my maids opened the door to the dining area, the noises inside quieted down and the ladies' attention were now on me.

I hate being the center of attention so I quickly went over to an empty spot next to the lady with beautiful brown hair. She looked over at me before giving me a big smile, showing her dimples. I envy those with dimples, it makes a person look a lot more charming.

"Greetings, I am Lee Hyerin. You seem to be around my age, are you also here for the selection?" she waited for my answer expectedly with her brown doe eyes.

"Nice to meet you Lady Hyerin, I am Han Goeun. I just arrived here today." I examined the girl infront of me and my, she was really a beauty. Her face was small and her hair was in a half up half down style. She gave off a warm aura with her outgoing personality.

"Let's not be so formal with one another. I do need another friend and I think me and you could get along really well." I nodded at her and was relieved on how smoothly she could come up with things to say to keep the conversation going.

Sitting next to her made me feel a little self conscious so instead, I put my focus on the food in front of us. There were so many different things to eat and I didn't know which one to pick up first.

Once I was full, I said my farewells and headed back to my room to get a goodnights rest. All the travelling made me feel more tired than I usually am and this girl needs her sleep. After washing up and getting my hair cared for, I sent my maids out for today.

I sat down in front of the mirror to get a good look at myself. I saw a girl with straight dark hair looking back at me and I sighed. Most people say I give off a cold aura due to my sharp features, especially my eyes. That is why I envy those with soft features and pretty round eyes.

Even if I dont get chosen, I hope they will welcome me back happily. You can get through this Goeun-ah.

With a determined face, I strode to my bed and was about to get in the covers before I heard my door being opened in a rush. A whish of cold wind entered my room and the door was shut as quickly as it was pushed open.

I was about to scream when the man wearing a face veil shushed me in the process. He was giving me a look of "make a sound and you're dead"

I quickly wrapped a thin robe around myself and grabbed a small object that's the size of my fist from on top of my drawer. I slipped it in my sleeves in case I needed to haul it at that man. As a woman, I wasn't taught any fighting or self defense moves so I'll have to just make use of my surroundings.

The man was in front of the door leaning in to hear if there was any footsteps outside. I desperately wished for someone to walk by and just get me out of this situation.

"wh-who are you? You will be punished greatly if they hear that you barged in a noble lady's room like this" I mustered up the courage to talk to him with a trembling voice but all I got in return was silence. GreatA few minutes passed by and I was reciting all the prayers I had learned from mother in my head.

"Is anyone in there? May I open the door, miss. I have to do a quick inspection of the rooms around here" A deep mans voice from over the door knocked gently but his voice sounded rushed, almost impatient. Was that the voice of an angel? My prayers have finally gotten answered

As fast like the wind, the stranger was suddenly behind me and held a knife to my throat. I desperately tried to pull his hand away but to no avail. I felt chills down my spine as he whispered in my ear "tell him to not come in or I will slit this delicate neck of yours. Which would you rather choose?" I closed my eyes and my breath was hitched as I felt an anxiety attack coming.

Hiding you would get me killed and you will kill me at the end anyways. I have no choice to begin with.

I slid my hand under my sleeve and felt the sharp object that I hid a while ago. Opening my eyes, I made my decision. Here goes nothing...

I took it out and with all my strength I smashed it in the man's face behind me before yelling "COME IN!" at whoever that was behind the door. I ran to the direction of the door and prayed that the stranger behind me was still on the floor grunting in pain from the hit.

The door flew open and a man holding a sword came rushing in and looked around quickly to grasp the situation. Just like how the door flew open, I flew over behind him to protect myself from danger. "H-He came in my room all of a sudden and threatened me so I d-didn't know what to do" I struggled to come up with words to say and held onto the mans back shirt for reassurance.

"Stay outside for a minute my lady, I'll deal with him quickly" He took my hands from behind his back and lightly nudged me backwards. I took the cue and left the room quickly. There was quite a big ruckus inside but I believe he dealt with it quickly because he came out without any scratches.

I tried to look behind him to see what happened to that man but he blocked my view completely.

I looked up at him and finally took in his appearance as he looked straight back at me as well.

I didn't notice before but he was tall and had black hair and bangs that were slightly messy from him fighting in there. His eyebrows thick and eyelashes long, I almost got jealous of him. And those full lips-

"eh-ehem" He coughed a little and I came out of my senses and blushed at the indecent thoughts that were just consuming me right now. Should I lie to him and say I got hit in the head? what an embarrassment Han Goeun.

"Thank you for saving me.. Sir..?" "General" he replied and I swear I didn't think I had a thing for deep voices but it sounded sexy.

"And I don't think I was the one that saved you. You had done enough damage to him already." I swear I saw a glint of amusement in his eyes before he switched back to a stoic expression immediately.

"I'll call over my soldiers to take care of him but I recommend you to not go back in there for tonight. Yeah, I won't go back in even if you drag me by force

"Very well then. I will call my maids over and rest in another room for tonight. But before that, could you get me a blanket from inside. It's a little embarrassing.." I tried to cover myself up with the robe more and he, as if now taking in my appearance, turned around abruptly to retrieve a blanket.

Part 3

"Lady Goeun, we heard about the incident that occurred last night, are you okay? Are you hurt anywhere?" Lady Hyerin repeatedly checked my hands and my face for any injuries.

She was the first to come up to me when I came in the dining room this morning and I was grateful for that. "it was an unexpected turn of events but it was taken care of swiftly. You don't have to worry anymore" I gave her a smile and ushered her to sit down with the rest.

We all greeted each other again and I found some familiar faces. Although I couldn't remember all, the names that stuck out to me the most were Nari and Miyoung. I had met them at Lady Byeols residence when I went with mother.

As we were all finishing up our meal, the door slid open and Court Lady Choi came in gracefully. "Have all the meals cleared away, our first lesson begins today." Immediately, the maids came swarming in and in no time, the tables were clean and tidy. "I am sure you guys know the rules that are to be followed when in this selection. But let me go over it once more to stress the importance of it." She eyed all of us but no one dared to look back at her and instead, we kept our eyes down.

"The contestants will not be able to leave on her own accord. However she can be dismissed by the crown prince or the King himself, which will not be a pleasant experience."

"This is to be a fair match and any signs of cheating, sabotaging, or fighting will not be tolerated. Punishments will be handed out according to the degree of crime that has been committed."

"And lastly, although we are testing to see your level of skills and intelligence, the decision will ultimately be up to the crown prince himself. "

"So to wrap this up, I would like to thank you all for being here and I would like to wish you ladies good luck on the upcoming tests." "Now, shall we begin?"

Court Lady Choi clapped her hands and the maids came in once again. "We will begin a physical checkup and screening for today. A spouse for the crown princess has to be healthy, pure, and have no scars on her body. We will be recording it down in your charts as the first step of this process. Do not worry, it will all be done separately and privately, and our records shall not be leaked to anyone but me and if needed, the crown prince."

We all waited for our turns as the maids ushered a few ladies out at a time.

I knew I was going to go through this, but having them check my body like that makes me feel weird inside. Noble ladies take care of their skin very well and are treated like a delicate flower. And just as how they treat us, we are required to look and act like a flower. Delicate, beautiful, pure, and obedient.

Once everyone was done, we were all dismissed for today. She said we could have our own personal time to either go to the pavilions or rest in our rooms.

"It's just the afternoon and we came out of our rooms a few hours ago.." I muttered to myself as I wandered around the endless halls. I heard someone's running footsteps from behind me and quickly turned to see who it was. There stood Hyerin holding her knees as she was panting, stabilizing herself.

"What's with the rush Hyerin? Do you want to tag along with me?" I smiled at her holding her hand up to me to give her a minute. "I wanted to take you to this beautiful spot I found in the palace yesterday. Do you want to come with me?" she showed me her pearly teeth as she linked our arms together.

I don't know when we dropped formalities but it felt more comfortable to talk to each other casually. I also figured out that we were the same age, only I was a few months older.

"Then you can lead the way"

"Let's gooo" she put her other hand forward and eagerly led the way there

---

"Wow" I admit, the place she took me to was so beautiful. We walked along the bridge as we observed the nature around us. There was many water lilies floating above the lake and the cherry blossom trees surrounded both of our sides. Right ahead, I saw a sitting place that I fell in love with immediately.

"Let's go sit down over there. It's such a beautiful spot where we can see everything happening around us."

We sat in comfortable silence until I broke it first. "Hyerin, if you become the crown princess, do you think this place would make you truly happy?"

She pondered over this question and her eyes scanned the area before she smiled. "If this place can't make me happy, I'll just have to be the one that makes this a happy place."

I was in awe with her way of words and I smiled as well. "Have you ever met the crown prince before? All I hear is how handsome he is or how he's got both the looks and the brains."

"No I haven't, but the girls here say that he's an eye candy to look at. They saw him passing by and I swear one of the ladies said they saw the gates of heaven open."

We looked at each other before we fell into fits of laughter at how cringey that was. The rest of our afternoon passed by like that, with us telling our childhood stories and getting to know one another better.

Just as how we were surrounded by pretty flowers and cherry trees that day, our friendship slowly started to blossom beautifully.

Part 4

"The first round of selection will be targeting how well you know your etiquette as a noble lady and quite possibly, the crown princess. We will be observing how well you perform these tasks as we teach them to you starting today."

I gotta thank my mother for this one. She never allowed me to slouch even when I was tired. Once, she came in at night to check up on me and was horrified to see me sleeping with my mouth open. I somehow managed to get rid of that sleeping habit as well.

They observed us as we all practiced our postures by walking with heavy dresses. Then we demonstrated the proper manners when eating, like what utensil to pick, and how our elbows shouldn't be on the table.

They also wanted us to take a written test to see how well we know how to read and write.

For about a week, we woke up in the early morning and then came back to our rooms at night tired of the lessons we had to take.

By the end of it, some of the girls obviously looked bored or just worn out from all the things they wanted us to demonstrate. Seeing all the dejected faces, Court Lady Choi softly chuckled. "A crown princess must not show that she is displeased with a situation, and instead, persevere through it. On the good side, I have some news that shall bring your moods up. Once the results for the first round is over, you will all start to visit his highness twice a week to make the process go by even faster."

"Oh my" "we will spend time with his highness?" "My heart is already fluttering" the girls' chatters grew louder as the excitement suddenly buzzed everywhere.

"We will look through all the tests you submitted and the things we recorded, as well as the physical check ups, to see who gets eliminated. 15 will be eliminated from the 30 of you sitting here with me today."

Would I be happy to be eliminated? I suddenly had that thought and I somehow felt sad thinking about it. There are people here that make me want to stay for a little longer like Hyerin, maybe the mysterious crown prince, and that one general I met that night...

Oh my god, Goeun! Snap out of it! How could you be thinking of him when you guys only met one time for a brief moment. I shook away my thoughts and came back to reality.

"We took up most of your days so we are granting you a 3 day break. In those three days, we will be reviewing everything, so you guys are free to go." "Starting.. now" Court lady Choi smiled at how we all bowed before excitingly rushing out of the room.

"ahh, the fresh air of freedom" Hyerin walked beside me purposely taking a deep breath of air.

I played along with her smelling the air "I agree, the air feels a lot more crisp and rich." She playfully smacked my arm and we both started to laugh at how childish we were being.

"Lady Han Goeun?" I heard my name being called by a familiar deep voice and I turned my head around to see him again.

"General, what brings you here?" I was genuinely surprised that he personally came to seek me out.

"There are some private matters that I had to discuss with you" he looked between me and Hyerin and she seemed to sense that.

"I'll take my leave now, see you later Goeun." she gave me a small wave before going in the opposite direction from us.

"Do you want to talk about it here orr?"

"Let's go to your old room first. It's about that man from that night."

"oh" was all I could say as I saw him turn around and lead the way.

What was I expecting? Did I want him to invite me for tea and then confess his love for me at first sight? pfft

.....

Yeah, I secretly did

I struggled to catch up to him since he was walking way too fast for my pace. "I'm embarrassed to ask this but could you slow down a bit. I can't seem to catch up with you."

He stopped abruptly and I ran into his back with a thud, unable to stop myself in time.

"Sorry about that, I don't usually act like this" I embarrassingly said as I rubbed my nose from the impact.

"No, It's my fault" he started to walk again but in a slower pace, so I could walk next to him normally. I secretly took a side glance and saw that he was wearing a maroon color today.

I wonder how old he is, he looks pretty young to be a general..

Once he opened the door, I looked inside to see that it was completely empty. My maids had gotten all my stuff from this room and moved me to another one after that incident.

"So what happened general? Did that man escape or something?" I jokingly asked but seeing how he kept his serious expression, I gulped.

"You aren't serious right? the security here must be so tight to let someone like him to escape..."

"Yes, he escaped. But we intentionally let him go"

We stared at each other for a bit as I was trying to process that information. I tried to keep calm but the memories replayed in my head when that man held a knife to my throat.

His chilling voice as he threatened to kill me made me shudder. Once I came back to my senses I grabbed onto the generals arms without thinking. I shook him saying "Are you crazy? Why would you let an idiotic psycho go loose again?"

He seemed to be caught off guard by my actions but I only cared about my safety right now. Manners could wait.

"He was a man planning to murder his highness" that gives you more of a reason to put 3, no 4 more locks outside his cell or even killing him would be a reasonable option

"But you let him go?" "Intentionally at that?" My sarcasm could be noticed from a mile away but now I was rethinking on how he was even appointed as a general in the first place.

"In order to catch the bigger fish, we let go of a small bait" once he said that, everything seemed to click into place. oh, he wants to catch the person that gives orders to that man.

"I understand you want to catch the bigger fish but.." I smiled at the general "That small bait will surely kill me when he has the chance." "Just think about it, I smashed an heavy object at his face which led him to bleed badly. If he has the guts to kill a prince, I'm probably worth a mere pebble that he can shove away anytime he wants, dear general."

I didn't realize I was still holding onto his arms until I noticed our close proximity. Once I backed away, I was going to turn around and leave until he suddenly spoke

"We strengthened our palace guards so no one would be able to come in. And if it puts you at ease, I, will protect you if needed." I didn't think I would forgive someone that easily, but I guess I am an easy woman.

"Thank you, you saying that will certainly help me sleep better tonight." I made sure my sarcastic comment made it through his ears before bowing and taking my leave.

Part 5

For the remaining 3 days, all I did was eat delicacies and stay in my room. It's better to take precautions after hearing that a killer is on the loose. Hyerin was curious on what me and the general talked about but she didn't mention it. I was glad she didn't because I'm pretty sure the general would have my head first if I ever spoke about this matter to anyone. It's probably top secret.

I laid down in bed hugging my pillow while I looked up at the ceiling. Tonight might be my last night here in the palace which I have grown accustomed to. The results will be out tomorrow but I didn't feel like saying goodbye to this place.

With that thought, I wore a comfortable long dress before sneaking out to go look for the general. I noticed that the general is not seen in the palace during the day but he's always doing stuff around night time. I might as well say my farewells because you never know, I might have failed.

I walked outside and towards the spot where the general's work room is at. There were guards in front of the building and I told them to tell him my name so he can let me in. Once they did I slowly made my way inside.

His study room was quite spacious where there was 2 tables. one had a big map on it and the other had books and papers stacked up. There, I saw him working away, writing down things I wouldn't even try to understand.

"Greetings General" I bowed to show my respects but he didn't even bother looking up. I stood there for a minute thinking he would stop writing, so when he didn't, I grabbed a chair from the first table and dragged it to where he was sitting. As I sat down and made myself comfortable, he finally acknowledged my presence.

"Are you usually this nosy and comfortable around others Lady Goeun?" he stared at me with those captivating eyes and I had to break eye contact before I broke into a blush.

"Only with you" I smiled before scanning the papers in front of him. "Do you ever sleep? I always see you doing work or running errands in the evening"

"Why are you here? Do you need me to protect you while you sleep?" he smiled rather mischievously for the first time and I now get why those ladies said they saw the gates of heaven open when they saw the crown prince.

"..ehem.. I was just here to say goodbye" I circled my finger slowly around the smooth surface of the table as shyness took in. I can't believe I came here just to say that.

"Bye?" He furrowed his eyebrows in confusion.

"You know, since the results will come out tomorrow, I just wanted to be ready for it, just in case. You did help me back then and I thought it would be appropria.."

"You'll pass"

I suddenly stopped blabbering once I heard his voice. What does he mean by "You'll pass"?

"Did you secretly look at the scores? are you that powerful to be able to do that?"

"No, but considering you, you're probably smart enough to pass the first round." His words alone brought such reassurance in me, I felt confident again.

"But maybe not the second round" I bitterly scoffed as those words left his lips. He knew that stung me and I so wanted to wipe that annoying smug expression off of his face.

Okay then, two can play this game.

"I think I like your stoic expression better general. You look like one of those scary clown masks right now"

With the sweet taste of victory, I said my goodnights and left his room.

Mother would probably hate how I am acting around him. But, why does it feel so... nice?

Morning came and all of us were gathered together waiting for Court Lady Choi to come in. Hyerin was holding my hand out of nervousness. The other ladies either pretended to act fine while some were nervously fiddling around. There was a weird tension in the air that no one had the guts to break.

The door creaked open and in came Court Lady Choi carrying a single slip of paper that held the fate of all of us sitting here.

"Everyone stand up" she said and we all obeyed quietly.

"When I say your name, you can sit back down" Would the names being called mean that you succeeded? or is it the other way around?

"Kwon Nari"

"Kim Yooseul"

"lim seyoung"

The more names she called out, the more nervous I became inside.

"Han Goeun"

I sat down after my name was called but still held Hyerin's hand. Once her name was called, I let out a breath that I didn't know I was holding. I don't know if it was a good thing if our names were called but we were much happier to be together.

Once she finished reading the 15 names from the list, Court Lady Choi looked up and around the ladies that were still standing.

"Unfortunately, those who are standing, did not pass the first round"

I heard a few burst out in tears while some shook in anger.

"You all did amazing here and I'm proud of every single one of you. You will all make amazing wives to your future spouses and become better role models to the people out there. I hope you aren't too sad to hear this news today. You have a whole life ahead of you, so hold your chins up and walk out of here proudly, not thinking that you failed, but that you succeeded in trying."

Her words made me feel emotional as I felt sad to see them leave as well. The girls were all very nice and I guess I grew fond of them in such a short amount of time. Once the girls all standing left to pack up, I looked around the room once again.

15..

Part 6

"The second round will immediately begin as of now. Today will be the first day that you guys will meet with the crown prince himself. Get to know one another, and if he takes a liking to you, you have a greater chance of passing to the last round in 2 weeks."

"By the names that I called you with, that is the order that you will meet his highness. Any questions?" Court Lady Choi looked around but seeing how we all stayed silent, she took that as a no.

"Kwon Nari, you're the first to go." I looked at Nari as she got up in a rush and left with a goofy smile on her face. The maids were to escort her to wherever his highness was at.

Hyerin leaned over to me before saying "If there's 15 of us and we get to meet him for 30 minutes each, how long would that be all together?"

"It would be about 8 hours"

I thought about it..30 minutes is probably very little time for us but his highness will have to sit for about 7-8 hours in total. By the time he's done, he would probably be so exhausted.

We were given permission to leave and spend the rest of our day off until we got called over. I was probably the 8th one to be called so I had a while till they would come to get me. I went back to my room and took out my embroidery supplies and a good material to start it off with.

"hmm now.. what to embroider.." I thought carefully before getting to work. Jasmine flowers would be a beautiful design on a handkerchief.

The rest of my time went by, with me perfecting my piece and bringing those flowers alive through my work. I was so into it that I didn't notice the maids coming in to fetch me.

"Lady Goeun, you shouldn't keep his highness waiting" I abruptly looked up processing those words before struggling to stand. Sitting in one position for hours made my feet go numb. As we walked to the prince's study room, I tried to gather my thoughts as my brain suddenly went blank. What am I even supposed to say to him?

Before long, the doors opened and I quietly made my way inside. I saw him at his table but he wasn't necessarily working. He was laying his head down and... sleeping? Just great, am I even allowed to wake him up?

I paced around the room and tried to make my footsteps louder or I tried putting a nearby book down a little harder so he could wake up on his own, but to no avail.

"hmph" I sat down across from him and quietly peeked at his sleeping face. He was handsome, but somehow, my heart didn't flutter at the sight in front of me.

Once I took a closer look, I noticed the dark circles under his eyes. I looked around his table to find some ink and paper. Once I did, I wrote him a small note before taking my leave.

Once out, I informed the girls outside to get some tea that helps with fatigue and deliver it to him.

"We can meet each other next time, your highness" I smiled before making my way back to my room.

Once Hyerin's turn was over, she ran into my room in the speed of lightning and had an obvious blush on her face.

She sat down next to me before squealing and smacking my arm multiple times. "Oww, Hyerin you don't have to hit me, I'm all ears." I put the needle down and put all my attention on her.

Flashback Hyerin's POV:

My hands were a little sweaty as I made my way inside. The study room was beautifully decorated and I fell in love with the amount of books there were in here. "Greetings your highness, thank you for giving me some of your time" once I said that, he looked up and I swear I think time stopped.

He had Black hair neatly pulled up and light brown eyes that were staring back at mine. He had a defined jawline and even his Adams apple looks sexy..

Hyerin, get a hold of your emotions! I blushed hard and lowered my head.

"Are you just going to stand over there? Come over here and sit down, my lady." he gestured me over to sit down across from him. Once I did, all the things I had prepared myself to say flew out the window.

I glanced up at him and almost choked on my spit seeing him staring at me with his elbows on the table and his hands supporting his chin. "What's your name?" his melodic voice somehow helped me to calm down and before I knew it, I was smiling back at him.

"It's Lee Hyerin, how about you your highness?" I copied how he was sitting and waited for his answer.

If anyone saw us from afar, they would think we are lovers from the close proximity. We were both sitting crisscrossed on the ground and his table was pretty low and small, befitting for only one person's use.

"Its Jong Yul, Hyerinssi"

(Ssi is a form of respect when put in a person's name. its pronounced as shi)

"Nice to meet you Jong Yulssi. What have you been working on this whole time?"

Just like that, my 30 minutes whizzed away as we naturally kept the conversation going.

"Bring in my dinner" Prince Yul motioned for his maids to bring in his meal, so I thought it was the cue for me to leave.

"Have a good meal your highness. I'll be taking my leave now." When I was getting up, I suddenly got pulled back down. He had grabbed my hand to pull me down but he wasn't letting go?!

"Who said you could leave without my permission?" I tried to come up with something to say but I guess my brain stopped working. We had a mini staring contest and I broke it off when I heard the maids bringing in his meal.

Am I supposed to just wait for him to finish eating? But the food looks soo good..

As I was having an inner battle with myself, I felt something cold being placed in my hands. When I looked up, there was a pair of chopsticks in my hand that Prince Yul was holding just a minute ago.

"Eat with me before you go" How can I not start to fall for him when he was being such a gentlemen.

"Just one bite then." I said as I looked at the food displayed in front of us. I guess I didn't keep my promise because one bite turned into me finishing half of the food with him.

Part 7

Later that night, I was suddenly called over by the crown prince himself.

"He is requesting your presence in his room, Lady Goeun." I stared wide eyed at my maid in front of me not believing her words.

I hesitantly got up and followed silently. Am I in trouble? I knew I shouldn't have written that darn note to him.

When I came in, I immediately bowed and greeted him.

"So you are Lady Han Goeun?" I could hear the amusement in his tone and that's when I knew I messed up.

"Did I hurt your feelings your highness?" I debated on whether I should dart out the room or sit down across from him.

"Your note did leave a lasting first impression." "You're boring your highness.. Have a good rest, and drink the tea when you wake up"

"It sounded both distant and close at the same time. And since we didn't get our 30 minutes, why don't I make it up for you right now" he gave me his best smile so I knew I had no choice but to come and sit down.

"Has your royal highness not gotten much sleep lately?"

"You can call me Prince Yul. Royal highness sounds too formal" I took a mental note of that.

"There's just been a lot of work piled up these past few days, and an annoying pest had come in my palace in that time."

Oh, he's talking about that man from that one night.

"Then why don't you enjoy the time you have now and sleep? There was no need to call me over since I wouldn't complain about it being unfair" I patted my hands on the cushions and he started laughing.

"You're so eager to push me away, why is that?"

I seriously thought about it..

"It's because I don't think I am fit to be a crown princess. There are many other women here that would be fitting for it. And I believe one woman has already piqued your interest?" I arched my eyebrow in expectation and I swear I saw his ears turn red.

"What makes you think that it's not you?" he suddenly asked that making me choke on literal air.

"What kind of women are you interested in, your highness?" Let's see if he really likes me or not.

"Someone who will be my light as I venture on in this dark world all alone." His words were rather cringe but it made me think of one person clearly.

"If you want a woman like that, I'll sincerely suggest someone for you. Lady Hyerin is an amazing woman, but I think you already know that." he tried to clear his throat and I broke out into laughter.

"I'll be taking my leave now, see you around, Prince Yul." As I was about to leave, he suddenly spoke up.

"Let's be friends Lady Goeun. Although I need a wife, I also need loyal people on my side when I become King."

I smiled before replying "I'll think about it"

A week and a half passed by and we were to meet the crown prince again. I heard he got busy last week so we didn't see him for the second time like it was scheduled.

All the ladies dressed up in their finest clothes and put makeup on to try to flatter his highness. We were informed that we would go in pairs of 2 and one group would consist of 3 people since there is 15 of us. Of course I chose Hyerin and she chose me.

Hyerin wore a pretty light purple dress and I wore a navy blue one. When it was our turn, we didn't head to the study room but instead, came out to the pavilion. He was sitting there enjoying his tea as we strode over to him.

"Good afternoon ladies, come sit down."

I quietly sat and looked at our surroundings. "I guess you got tired of being in your room, Prince Yul."

He nodded and looked at the sky. "And the weather is especially beautiful today, it would be a waste to stay indoors."

I drank my tea since I didn't know what else to say to him. What do you say to a person you met only a few times?

Hyerin cleared her throat and spoke up "Do you want to take a walk your highness? This could be our last time meeting one another and I think a stroll would be nice." Something flickered in his eyes as she said that but he quickly changed back to his usual smiling self.

"Shall we go then?"

We were sitting just fine in the shade Hyerin-ah, Why make us walk now?

I stood up lazily but kept my composure. As we all walked side by side, Prince Yul and Hyerin went into their own little world. I looked around and a familiar person caught my attention.

Its been a while since I've seen him, I kind of miss talking to him.

He was on the other side of the lake practicing his archery with his men. I observed them quietly as we walked, focusing on how accurate the general's aiming was. I take back what I said when I asked myself how he even became the general. He has the skills and the intelligence.

Watching him was a lot more interesting than listening to what the other two was talking about. I think Prince Yul saw where I was looking at because he suddenly spoke to me catching me off guard "Are you interested in archery Lady Goeun?"

I was taken aback by what he asked since I didn't realize that they caught me staring. "haha, I enjoy watching it but wouldn't dare to hold one in my hands. Like any other lady, I'm interested in painting, embroidery, and going to festivals." I looked over at them and I saw him nodding his head.

Hyerin's eyes also shined and she immediately linked our arms together. "If neither of us passes, should we go to the festival together Goeun? I heard this year, it would be really grand and beautiful."

"Yeah, lets do that. I'll buy you all the food you want to eat, Hyerin-ah." We laughed together recalling how Hyerin said she loves food a lot.

"You both must be close" We turned around and saw Prince Yul looking amused at the situation.

Hyerin leaned her head on my shoulder. "She's like my older sister now" I smiled at her and then looked at the crown prince.

Jealous much?

He cleared his throat before turning to Hyerin "Don't say that you won't pass though. We could all go to the festival together one day"

I softly chuckled

As he walked in front of us, I heard him muttering to himself "I'll make sure of it." I glanced over at Hyerin as we walked together side by side.

Yeah, I'll make sure she passes too

Part 8

"Today will conclude the end of the second round of selection. Out of the 15 of you, with the help of the crown prince, we have chosen the 6 that will move on."

The dreaded day came where the 9 of us will go home. I don't even know how I survived this far but if I get eliminated today, I would still be happy with the results.

"Lee Hyerin"

"Yoo Bora"

"Kwon Nari"

"Cho Sun-hi"

"Han Goeun"

"Song Ji-young"

The girls that got called were glowing with happiness while the rest were crying in despair. Court Lady Choi sighed before starting her intellectual speech again.

I don't think it was a good thing to be selected for the third round. I already told the prince I wanted to be just friends, so why am I still here?!

"The third and final round will determine our crown princess, so his highness himself gave out a question he wants you ladies to try and answer. The answer will be due in a week, so submit your letters to me after thinking hard about it." Court Lady Choi gave each of us a slip of paper before leaving to do her other work.

The question was simple but I don't think it would be that easy to answer.

"How can I make my people happy as the crown prince of this nation?"

I had a whole week to write down my answer so I didn't rack my brain like how the other girls were doing. Hyerin said she already had something in mind, which I wasn't surprised of, because she has her way with words as well.

It was around 11 am in the morning and I was bored out of my mind. Hyerin pulled me to the side a while ago and told me that Prince Yul wanted to meet her in the royal library today privately.

I parted ways with her a while ago and walked around aimlessly. Before I knew it, my feet had led me to the general's work room. "Is he inside?" I asked the soldiers but they shook their heads no.

I wonder where he could be at this time?

I walked to that one place I saw where the general was practicing archery with his men. I had a mission to accomplish today and I won't back down until I succeed.

Once I went to the training area, I saw all the men wielding their sword and the general himself watching over it from the side, giving out advices on what to improve.

"General?" I called out in a whisper shout voice from afar hoping that he heard me. He finally noticed me once I waved in his direction. His hair was up in a bun today and his bangs were swaying softly by the wind.

"Lady Goeun, what brings you here?" Now that I think about it, I'm always the one seeking him out to meet up with him and spend time together. Am I being annoying?

"Nothing really, I just wanted to see if you had any free time today. I was bored and didn't have anyone to hang out with.." I stared at him expectedly waiting for his answer.

He sighed and ran his hand through his bangs. "I unfortunately don't have time to do that right now. I'm training my soldiers and am also dealing with the man who escaped a while ago." He had lost a little weight from the last time I saw him and it made me feel concerned.

"Okay you don't have to hang out with me for long. Just take a small rest in the shade here." I pulled him away from the heat and into the shade so he could sit down and relax.

"Here, I think I have it with me right now." I pulled out the handkerchief I had recently finished and tried to wipe the sweat from his forehead. Just as I was about to pull away, he suddenly held on to my wrist stopping me from moving.

"W-what are you doing?" Flustered, I tried to free myself from his grasp but he wouldn't budge an inch. Instead he pulled me closer to him and I let out a small gasp. I've never been this close to a man before..

"That's what I want to ask you. Why are you, the crown prince's woman, looking after another man? Or are you like this to all of the men here?" His eyes were cold and distant, his warm breath fanning my face. His voice sounded irritated and that made me feel hurt inside.

"Who said that I was the crown prince's woman? The results aren't out yet and I even told his highness that I wasn't interested" "And no, I am not that undignified or desperate to care for every man with affection" By the end of my speech, I felt out of breath and angry with the man in front of me.

We stared at each other silently for a moment, his gaze was unexplainable and fierce, but I had no reason to back down.

Today didn't turn out the way I had imagined it..

His grip on my wrist loosened and I harshly pulled away before holding the spot that turned red from the pain.

"All I wanted to do was ask for your name today. Is it that bad that I want to get closer to you?" I looked down slowly and my brain was chanting in my head Do not cry, do not cry, don't let him see your tears

"Are you perhaps interested in me, Lady Goeun?" This time he gently held my wrist that was at my side and rubbed it softly, easing the pain.

"I don't deserve to have a woman like you caring for me" He tilted his head to the side to take a closer look at me. I pouted slightly before raising my head. "So you won't even give it a try?"

"Then let's take it back a few steps and start over. My name is Kim Yo Han, and you are?"

At least he didn't fully reject me

I found my smile again and made a little courtesy.

"It is nice to meet you, Kim Yo Hanssi, I am Han Goeun"

I liked how his name sounded and thought it matched him really well.

I wished that he knew, that he was the reason why I embroidered jasmines on that particular handkerchief.

(If you don't already know, feel free to search up the meaning of jasmine flowers:))

Part 9

"**B**ring me some paper and ink"

  I had 2 days left to submit my letter and I think I finally found my answer. I dipped my brush into the ink and held my sleeve up before beginning to write.

Before you start reading, I am simply writing this as a fellow friend and a loyal subject of this nation. How can you make your people happy as the crown prince of this nation? First thing's first, you shall start by actually making them "your" people, your highness. Yes, you are the crown prince, but they only recognize you as someone they can't see or touch. You are on a different level from them. You have to start gaining their trust and increase their love towards the royal family. If someone with power and wealth steps in one day and offers them gold, riches, and a place to stay, they would move away from your side in a heartbeat. To make these people happy, do your part faithfully as the crown prince and the future king of this nation. Look through those that supposedly work by your side and pull out the thorns that is in the way of your success. Think from the peoples' perspectives and living conditions, and seek out into the world to find out the problems they might be facing against. That is what will make them happy, and in return, you will have the people on your side.

Satisfied with my work, I folded the paper carefully before venturing out to find Court Lady Choi. I don't think I would be reassured if I sent my maid out to deliver this. Once I found her, I gave it to her before going to look for General Kim.

We've been hanging out lately after my little confession but he insists on drawing the line between us.

I so far figured out that he is turning 22 years old and his birthday is during the early winter time. He seems to be pretty closed off when I ask him about his childhood or his adolescent years, so I decided to not touch on that subject anymore.

If someone told me that in a span of a month, I would fall head over heels for a man I barely know, I would've straight up laughed at their face.

Love really does change people

As I turned the corner, I saw 2 familiar ladies grabbing each other's hair and yelling at one another. Their dresses were wrinkled and a mess, their hair tangled up in each other's hands. "Who said you could peek at my written answer, you cheater!" The lady in green attempted to push the one in orange away but failed.

"HOW AM I A CHEATER?! I already submitted my work to the Court lady already"

"YOU LIAR! I clearly saw you snooping around my room a few days ago as well!"

Their bickering went on and on and I covered my face out of second hand embarrassment. Should I call Court Lady Choi or the guards over?

Maybe I should just turn around and pretend it never happened. It's not my business anyways, it's better to let them get all their anger out. I attempted to walk away when a hand suddenly blocked my way.

"Are you seriously about to walk away without helping them?" Surprisingly, the one I expected to see the least was right in front of me.

I bowed down before saying my greetings. "Crown prince Yul, what brings you here?"

"I ran over here hearing all this noise and my my- it's quite a sight seeing noble ladies acting like this." He arched his eyebrow and stared at the commotion.

"Those noble ladies are quite possibly your future women, so if someone has to stop it, you're the perfect candidate." "Good day" I stepped out of the way and walked in the opposite direction gracefully. I choose who I want to help, I don't come running in just for anyone.

I suddenly felt bad for my mother who taught me to always be respectful to everyone. I guess once a bird leaves its nest, they are all on their own. It's been a month since I have been away from home but I truly just began to explore the depth of myself as a person. I didn't know I had the ability to joke around and be childish with my friends. I also didn't know that I could be soft to the people I care about but be tough when unavoidable situations occurred.

Home felt foreign now, where I was constantly watched by the eyes of my parents and maids. I remember one night I wanted to just sit down and have a nice late night talk with mother. When I was at the entrance of her room, I heard quiet whispers from the other side of the door.

"Tell me all the things she did when she went out today alone. Who did she meet, how did she act, and what did she do before coming home. Don't leave out a single detail." I heard mother's hushed voice as she demanded the other person to speak.

As I heard the other person talk, I recognized their voice almost immediately and shock coursed through me. I was horrified to find out that one of my closest maids, Iseul was busy serving me and reporting all my movements to mother every single day. From that day on, I hired a maid on my own and kept her by my side. Areum was the only person I trusted out of all the maids in that household.

Don't get me wrong, I don't despise my parents. However, there's a limit to being over protective than being downright obsessed. Her actions clearly told me that she was obsessed with controlling me and how I am as a person. Father only followed his wife's words and wouldn't dare disobey them. I think I grew up to be a decent woman, but mother raised me in an unhealthy way. She has already done enough damage and I am now slowly starting to fix them.

But once I go back home, she will probably be more strict on me than ever before because I would have failed her.

Part 10

Chapter 10: 3rd person POV

"Here are all the letters, your highness. We will all leave it up to your judgement. Whatever decision you make, we will accept whole heartedly." Court Lady Choi handed the papers to Prince Yul before making her way out of his study room.

He scanned through the names and once he found the one he was looking for, he eagerly opened it, as if he was receiving a present. Her beautiful writing was neat and no mistakes could be seen.

Lee Hyerin

Greetings Jong Yulssi, when I heard the question that you provided for us, I think I immediately thought of an answer for you. As the crown prince of this nation, you probably feel like there's a heavy burden on your shoulders. You are always expected to have an answer for the peoples' problems. In order to help your people and make them happy, I believe that you should achieve that happiness first. Once you get a taste of how it feels to be happy, you will want to share it with the rest of the world. Doing your duty as the crown prince would not feel like an unbearable job to you, but instead, be a privilege to help those in need with your own hands. How do you attain happiness, you say? It must sound really selfish for me to write this, but having the right people by your side. If I ever become the crown princess, I promised myself that I would not make his highness suffer all alone. I would carry your burdens with you by your side and try to make the best decisions for the people. That way, your people would be happy, but you also, would share that happiness with them.

Jong Yul put the paper down before letting out a soft sigh. "I knew it was her from the beginning. I don't think I want to read the rest anymore"

"That won't be fair for the others then. At least pretend to read them before choosing." A voice came from the door and Prince Yul looked up before holding his chest jokingly. "Atleast make your footsteps known before coming in. I think I got a heart attack"

General Kim Yo han stood at the door with a mischievous glint in his eyes. "I even coughed a few times but you were too smitten by a certain letter." As he made his way over to sit down, Yul rubbed his neck embarrassingly before opening the rest of the letters.

"Here's Lady Goeun's letter.. She was also really interesting to talk to." Yul suddenly turned quiet as he read the words she had carefully wrote. "First make them "my" people..." "She is very poetic but realistic at the same time. A rare gem compared to most ladies." He reread her letter again before clapping enthusiastically.

"She is worthy of being my friend. Should I introduce her to you? You two would make a great match" He eyed his best friend sitting across from him while wiggling his eyebrows playfully.

"There's no need. We've already met" General yo han let out a small smile but it vanished faster than it had appeared. "But you already know I can't do-"

"I know I know but are you seriously going to throw away your whole life waiting for her?" Yul shook his head disapprovingly before looking up at his friend's stoic face.

"You've waited enough. It's been years Yo han. It's time to forget" Yo han felt a lump in his throat but he immediately regained his composure realizing how vulnerable he was being.

"I have news on the man who we let free intentionally. He had not been revealing anything so far but my men has noticed a strange movement by him a few nights ago. He made a visit to Minister Pyo's residence and has been untraceable since then. What do you suggest we do? Shall I investigate further?"

Something flashed in Yul's eyes as minister Pyo's name was mentioned. Goeun's letter suddenly came to mind.. "Look through those that supposedly work by your side and pull out the thorns that is in the way of your success."

"I want full reports on this by the end of the week. Make sure to put a tail on the minister, his people, and try to find the man that went into hiding. That is all."

General Kim bowed his head before making his way out of the room.

With newfound determination in his eyes, Prince yul grabbed Hyerin's letter before going out to find Court Lady Choi.

My life has been way too bitter, I think it's time to add a little bit of sweetness to it.

He smiled at Lady Choi before handing the letter in her hands. "Now, you have your crown princess. Make sure to announce it first thing tomorrow."

That done. Now to go see father and mother. Yul rubbed his temples before making his way to his majesty's room.

Part 11

We all stood side by side and kept our heads low as we were in the presence of his majesty and the queen. Prince yul was sitting next to them, with a proud grin on his face.

It was so painfully quiet as I fiddled with my dress waiting for them to announce the results. I looked over at Hyerin to see what she was doing and found her taking small peeks at Prince Yul.

He also seemed to be looking at her happily, obviously giving us the answer.

Court Lady Choi came in and bowed to his and her majesty before bowing to Prince Yul. Afterwards, she faced towards us before calling out 1 name.

"Everyone except Lee Hyerin can leave this room now" I smiled at Hyerin who was kind of trembling before rubbing her back soothingly.

"You guys have about a day to pack up all that you need and leave the palace. I am very grateful for the time we have spent together this past month. I wish you all a good luck in your lives ahead." We all bowed before taking our leave.

Once the door closed, 2 girls burst into tears while the 2 others silently left to their rooms. I also went to my room and sat down quietly. My maids started to pack my stuff and I suddenly felt really sad to part like this. Watching clothes being packed left and right, the news finally dawned on me.

I wiped my tears silently not understanding why I was crying this much. With my eyes puffy and nose red, I stepped outside to get some fresh air.

I guess that was an excuse because I was actually looking for General Kim, to say goodbye to him. Once I'm out of the palace, we won't see each other much, or maybe even none at all. I walked through the usual path to the training area that I practically memorized already. Once I arrived, to my disappointment, he wasn't here.

"Where is your general?" I asked one of his men and all they said was "He left to go outside the palace since last night."

"When do you think he'll be back? I had something to say to him." I looked at them with a sense of desperation and they seemed to notice.

"I don't know my lady. He didn't say"

"oh, okay then. Have a good day"

I dejectedly went back, my mood worse than before. When I made it to my room, it was completely empty and my maids had already packed my stuff. "Thank you for helping me during my stay here. I would like to gift you a jewel each, what do you say?" Scanning my bags, I found the small wooden box that had many different necklaces, bracelets, and other jewelry inside.

"No, no it won't be necessary Lady Goeun. It was a pleasure serving you" I still took out a jewel and hair accessories and gave it to the both of them.

They bowed before smiling at me gratefully. I could see how their eyes were shining in happiness. It would be a pity to not give them anything for all the hard work I put them through here.

I had my meal served in my room today because I didn't feel like conversing with anyone at the moment. I don't think any of the ladies would want to do that anyways. Hyerin is still probably busy greeting people and moving over to a temporary place to stay before her ceremony. There she will have to learn the things that need to be taught before she becomes part of the royal family. This marriage would take about 2-3 months of preparing before they actually get officialy married. It all sounds like a big headache to me. Good luck Hyerinah.

After eating till I was full, I pulled out a piece of paper from the table drawers and began to write.

Dear General Kim, have you come back to the palace yet? I heard that you're really busy at the moment and left for some business outside. It's a pity that we couldn't say our farewells to one another before I left. Do you remember that time where you comforted me when I thought that I wouldn't pass the first round? I went to say goodbye then as well, But I guess this time, it's for real now. You should still keep the promise of protecting me though. But if you don't want to, then just make sure to catch that man soon. Take care of yourself and visit me from time to time. See you soon, then?

I delivered it to his work room and left it on his table.

Once I was about to go in the palanquin, rushing footsteps were heard from behind me.

"Goeun Unniee" "Waitt!" (Unnie means older sister). I turned around to see Hyerin running towards me and a few ladies trying to stop her.

She came crashing into me pulling me in for a hug. "Our crown princess shouldn't be running like that" I parted with her and saw how she was teary eyed.

"Make sure to write letters to me often. I want you to come to the ceremony, I'll make a special request myself."

"Ooo, you're using your powerful status already, just for me" We both laughed and I hugged her again. "Take care of yourself, and if the crown prince is a jerk to you, tell him that Goeun Unnie will haul her shoe at his head" She laughed but nodded her head.

The palanquin slowly took off and I tried to leave without any regrets in my heart. It took us a while to get home, and when it was put down, my heart felt like it went down as well. I got off nervously, waiting to see how my parents would react.

"Welcome home my child" father stood there with a smile on his face and I let out a sigh of relief.

"Where's mother and brother?" I looked around but no one else was at the entrance.

"Your mother is inside but won't come out of her room. And your brother is out there, travelling near and far again." Father smiled sadly and I nodded before making my way inside the house.

"Mother, I am home." I slowly entered her room but an object was suddenly thrown at the wall making me yelp in surprise.

"Don't show your face to me anymore. none of you" I was left speechless by how she was acting. "My only son leaves his family and travels to wherever he wants. I don't even know what he's up to and wouldn't even know if he turns up dead somewhere."

I stood quietly trying to comfort my pitiful mother. My older brother, Han hyunwoo, suddenly told us of his dream to travel around the many nations. Mother, accepted it, thinking he would come back in a few months or so. She loved her son too much to say no to him, and here are the consequences. He comes back a few times a year, once every few months.

He never tells us where he's been and is very secretive about his journeys. I try to understand him, but his actions, made mother become obsessed with me. Although I love him, there's times where I despise his decisions.

"My only daughter goes to a selection and passes 2 rounds, giving me false hope. But nope, she comes back at the end with nothing. Both of you are failures." she spit out her words venomously with anger in her eyes.

I know she was lashing all her anger out on me, but I am not made of steel.

"It's nice to be welcomed back so warmly, mother." Feeling the tears brimming in my eyes, I turned around and went straight back to my room. A nap will take away all the pain, Goeun. Forget about it and go to sleep. With tears rolling down my eyes, I forced myself to sleep and escape from reality for just a little bit.

I somehow ended up in a peaceful village where the sky was clear and the rivers were flowing gently. Kids were running around in joy and a cheerful atmosphere was created.

People were busy with their own lives, mothers tending to their kids and fathers helping their wives and easing their troubles. Everyone seemed content with their lives as I observed them quietly from the sidelines. Glancing to my left, I studied the man beside me trying hard to etch his appearance into my head.

I was walking down the long road with him, not minding my aching legs. Cherry blossoms were falling down slowly as I interlaced our hands together, afraid that he would leave me if I blink my eyes.

He smiled at me so warmly and tenderly, with love filled in his eyes.

Part 12

3 months later

3 months passed by and everyone had things to accomplish, whether it was plans on getting married or attending someone's birthday. Everyone was busy, but my time felt like it was slowed down to a stop. Nothing felt exciting anymore, the same routine every single day. I became robotic due to mother's constant nagging and just stayed in my room majority of the time.

The only times I was happy was when Hyerin sent me a letter during her busy schedules. She kept me up to date on what was happening around the palace. She said they caught the people that tried to harm his highness a few weeks ago. Her ceremony was also around the corner and our family was invited. Mother suddenly began to treat me better hearing that I was friends with the crown princess.

The general never wrote back to me nor did he visit me in the span of 3 months. Being the stubborn self that I am, I didn't attempt to write back to him either. The first month, I waited for his letters everyday, because that was the only thing I looked forward to. The second month, the realization that I was forgotten seeped in. And now the third month, I finally accepted the sad reality. But being the pathetic fool that I am, I still miss him.

"Lady Goeun, would you like to go shopping for a new dress? We could go look at the fabrics store and then get one custom made for you" Areum looked through my closet and reorganized them so that I had lighter dresses to wear. This year's summer was pretty tiring, with the heat rising to an all time high and the blazing sun shining over the buildings, making everything hot to touch. I should get a few more dresses and some face veils too.

With that thought, I sprung up and startled poor Areum along the way. "Let's go then!"

Areum cheered loudly and ushered me to sit down so she can fix my hair. I played around with the long strands of my hair and then put on a thin face veil before standing up.

Once we went outside, I walked through the markets and looked at all the fabrics they had displayed. Picking out the light purple fabric and the white one, I handed the money before carrying on to the next place.

"I want the bottom of the sleeves to have small but delicate flowers embedded on them and the sleeves to be long and flowy. And could you make the purple fabric the inner dress and the white would be the outer. Then with the remaining purple fabric, could you make a pretty belt with it?"

I drew a light sketch before handing it to the lady that makes my dresses.

"ah- yes, I'll finish it in a few days and have it delivered to your residence" She bowed before taking the fabrics from Areum's hands.

Areum and I then went to eat some delicious snacks before coming back home. Confusion washed over me seeing Lady Byeol, her husband and her son sitting with Mother and Father. They all had bright smiles on their faces which obviously meant bad news for me.

"Areum, let's sneak in through the back door. I refuse to hear whatever they are talking about" I hid behind Areum and was slowly retreating when mother's hawk-like eyes caught sight of me. Dang it

"Ah, there's my lovely daughter. She had some outside errands to run and came home a bit late." she gave me that one stare and I trudged over to them in defeat before greeting them.

I sat down and tea was served to me like usual. "Let's get straight to the point then, since we are all present. I would like the both of our families to join as one and have come to ask for your daughter's hand in marriage."

I totally expected this since I saw the son here as well. He flashed his flirty smile before eyeing me up and down. I felt disgusted by his stare but no one seemed to notice that.

Their son was known to be a player amongst all the ladies. Everyone knew who he was because of all the women he had flirted with, but his mother was the only clueless one. Or I guess she just pretended to not know about her son's doings.

He wasn't too shabby looking, but he wasn't my type. His personality was as foul as a bucket of animal manure.

Before mother had the chance to speak, I raised my chin up and spouted out whatever that came to my mind. "I'm sorry to say this, but my heart already belongs to another."

"Yes, her heart belongs to- wait what?" mother turned around swiftly, just processing my words.

They all stared at me in shock while I blinked my eyes innocently. Her hands trembling under the table, she gave me a what nonsense are you saying look. I don't even know what was spewing out of my mouth anymore either.

"My lover is a bit far away right now so we are writing through letters. Once he is done with his work, he promised to come here right away so we can begin our marriage preparations." I flashed them my most brightest smile and watched as the chaos unfolded in front of me.

"And kind sir, would you please stop staring at a taken woman's body like that. It is very undignified and rude." I covered my chest area and gave him a glare. Flustered, he coughed and gulped down his tea.

Mother stared at me horrified and Father was busy trying to calm her down. At this rate, she looks like she will faint. Lady Byeol and her family left quickly and I was nice enough to even walk them out of the door.

As I sat back down, mother gave me a sinister smile. "So you have finally lost your mind haven't you? How dare you lie with that innocent face of yours. You wench!" She tried to grab something from the table to throw at me, but my quick reflexes had left her with nothing. I grabbed all the teacups and brought it to my side. I'll protect you my babies

"Who is the man that you have been talking to behind our backs? What family is he from?" Father eyed me suspiciously and I let out a nervous giggle.

"You couldn't have possibly met someone before the selection so.." mother's eyes widened before she smacked my arm.

"You weren't allowed to be with other men during the selection, so what in the world happened?!!"

"I can't reveal his name but he's from a really good family"

"If you can't bring that man to me in under a month, I will agree to the marriage proposal that Lady Byeol's family offered. No exceptions." Mother made it crystal clear that she wasn't lying and father silently nodded next to her.

I looked over at Areum and she was silently waving at me, telling me with her eyes how much trouble I was in.

Oh boy, what have I gotten myself into

Part 13

As I entered the palace again, a wave of nostalgic feelings washed over me instantly. Memories I had made here were one of the best moments of my life.

The day came when Hyerin and Prince Yul would have their wedding ceremony and the Han family was invited.

Mother and father greeted everyone and I stood in the sidelines smiling politely at whoever was passing by. My eyes repeatedly scanned over the crowds, trying to find a certain man.

Once I looked over to my right, I saw a familiar figure in the distance leaning against the tree, staring right back at my direction. Or at least I think he was. My heart fluttered seeing him again after a long time. His hair had definitely grown a bit but he still looked the same compared to when I last saw him. He looked really dashing today wearing navy blue and I could tell he put in effort to look his best.

"I'll be back in a minute, father" I spoke to father in a hushed voice and he motioned for me to go, his attention on the elderly couple he was conversing with.

I walked towards him slowly, grabbing onto the hem of my skirt nervously. I had worn the light purple dress that I personally designed since it was a special day today. He suddenly stopped leaning and stood up straight, as if waiting expectedly.

I truly missed him. I missed everything about him, from his deep voice that softly spoke to me and to his smile that even appeared in my dreams. But what was this feeling that was overweighing that right now?

Maybe it was hurt, or anger, I wouldn't know. Did he even miss me? My throat was stinging and my heart ached dully, as I stared into that man's eyes.

I broke eye contact and stared straight ahead before walking right past him. If he wanted to lose contact with me, then fine, let's act like strangers then.

I barely took another step before I was turned around swiftly, catching me by surprise. Yo Han looked at me, probably trying to read through my thoughts.

I smiled before saying "Do I know you?"

He furrowed his eyebrows in confusion and kept a tighter hold of my hand. "Lady Goeun, what are you talking -" before he could finish whatever he was saying, I looked behind him and saw mother and father coming over to our direction with a weird smile on their faces.

I thought they were busy talking with the others, how did mother notice me gone so fast?

oh no The cogs in my brain turned wildly and a new plan was formed. Ohhoho

"Quick, act like my lover for a bit." I slid my arms in his before pleading with my eyes. "Tell my parents we plan to get married later in the future because you're busy at the moment" Yo han looked puzzled with the situation and I can understand him, I stranger zoned him one minute ago and now I'm asking him to be my lover. I probably sound like a psycho

"What did you get yourself into now?" He shook his head and I held onto his arms even tighter. "If you don't help me now, I will be forced to marry this pervert back at home."

"Is this your charm Lady Goeun? You first attracted a killer and now a pervert? What's it going to be next time?" He smirked and I smiled back at him. "Let's just say I have very bad luck when it comes to men."

"And what will I get out of helping you?" He raised his eyebrow in expectation and my mind went blank for a moment.

"I will accept this as a form of apology from you. The last 3 months... I won't question it" That was the best I could come up with since he doesn't really owe me anything.

Before he could speak, mother and father's footsteps were heard as they got closer to us.

"So this is your faraway lover that you were writing letters with?" Mother examined him before looking at our linked arms.

"Good evening, I hope your trip here wasn't difficult. I am General Kim Yo Han." He bowed and I stood amazed at how respectful he was acting.

"My my, you're respectful and handsome, so when are you planning to get married?" Mother straightforwardly asked and I covered my face in embarrassment.

"Mother there's things like self introductory and getting to know one another. You can't just ask suddenly like that" I looked over at Yo Han's face as he rubbed the back of his neck.

"As general, I have many things to do so I can't marry at the moment." He glanced over at me and I could tell he was slowly starting to lose it.

I gestured with my hands for him to breath in and out slowly.

"Let me speak with your parents for a little bit, let's get to know each other. After all, we will become in laws one day." Father looked at us expectantly and I let out a nervous laugh.

"hehe that won't be nesessary. I am just getting to know him better and I exaggerated a bit about getting married fast last time father." Yohan was stiff next to me and I realized my plan was starting to crumble horribly.

"Nonsense, lead the way, my son in law." Mother proudly patted him on the back and my blood ran cold. I think I messed up badly, and seeing Yohan's expression, I don't think I will make it out of here alive.

His parents were sitting patiently, sipping their tea quietly in the distance. I kept whispering "I'm sorry" "Don't kill me" and "I didn't think this would happen" to him over and over again but he stared straight ahead with his jaw tightened as we were walking in their direction.

Mother and Father greeted them politely before dropping the news to them as well. His mother stared at us in shock before standing up and walking towards Yohan and I. "Is this why you declined all those girls I showed you? You already had such a pretty one next to your side all this time."

I blushed without realizing and introduced myself.

His father also came to us before whispering to Yohan. I could hear them clearly since I was standing next to him. "Finally, I thought you would be stuck on that one girl forever" He patted his shoulder proudly, and I tugged at Yohan's sleeve trying to grab his attention.

I stared at Yohan in confusion but he kept his gaze straight ahead with a tight smile. Seeing that forced expression, a pang of guilt crept up to me. He already has a lover.

And I just ruined the chance of them being together.

Introducing your partner to your family is the same thing as saying that you want to get married to one another. I only meant to fake it to my parents but mother just had to go an extra step and rush things.

We left them to talk and they gladly shooed us off, immersed in their own conversation. I followed behind him quietly making sure my breathing wasn't even heard. Once he stopped walking, I backed away a few steps knowing what was about to come.

"Han Goeun" It was the first time he said my name fully, but his voice sounded stern and angry.

"Do you realize what you dragged me into?" "Do you think marriage is a joke?!" he turned around and I flinched back.

"I...I.." I couldn't form anything to say as an excuse so I kept my head low in shame. "Forgive me"

He sighed and ruffled his hair in frustration. "You will be unhappy in this marriage too. Because, your husband's heart will not belong to you entirely"

I sniffled softly and wiped away the tears that were forming. "I never asked for it to turn out this way either. Okay then, let's go back and fix this mess. I will apologize to your parents and beg them to not get mad at you. Then you can go back to whoever you guys were talking about. I'm sorry"

I hope my heart is okay after this. For 3 agonizing months, my heart ached in longing and now it's starting to crack and shatter into pieces. Grabbing his hand, I tried pulling him towards the direction of where our parents were at.

"But what about you then? I don't want you getting married off to that man you told me about" his words made me halt and I swear I almost grabbed his hair out of frustration.

"Why would you care?" I don't even know why I was getting mad at him when I'm the one at fault. "I am close enough to care about you and your wellbeing, Goeun"

I sat down on the grass before looking up at him. "Then what do you want me to do" Exhausted, I brought my knees to my arms and laid my head down. As I closed my eyes, I heard shuffling as he sat down next to me.

We stayed in silence for a bit and only the sound of the whishing wind was heard.

"Her name is Hwang Minah." He said rather softly.

"Your lover?" I kept my head in my arms not trusting myself as I failed to control my facial expressions.

He hummed in approval. "I promised that I would wait for her and that I would be willing to give up the world for her"

Looking up, I saw his sad smile making me feel like an extra horrible person. "Are you still waiting?" His eyes dilated for a moment and I saw the emotions swirling in his eyes. His lips slightly trembled, as if he was going to start crying.

"I don't know" was all he said before turning his head away.

How badly I want to be that woman, she took up all the space in his heart. But where could she be now?

I decided to not pry into his love life any longer, and made up my mind. "Give me just 1 month to clear this up. I'll tell them I broke it off because I fell out of love. Then we can go back to living our own separate lives."

"Jus-Just help me out for only today. Then you won't see even my shadow near you anymore" averting his gaze, I got up and dusted off my dress.

"I'm sorry" his low voice brought me to a stop and I chuckled softly.

"For what? Not playing pretend with me? Or not reciprocating the same feelings back? Please, don't make me feel even worse than I already am."

I put on a happy facade and regained my usual composure.

"Well then, let us go support our crown prince and princess's special day."

Part 14

The wedding ceremony was very formal and grand with decorations hung up everywhere. Varieties of food were set on the tables and alcohol was served one at a time.

Hyerin looked absolutely stunning wearing a long red dress with small gold designs on them. Her head piece looked heavy from here so I can't even imagine how she was feeling inside.

However, she looked unbothered by it as she and the crown prince gave their bows to one another and performed the royal customs for the ceremony.

I tried to feel happy just like everyone else, but the events from earlier kept replaying in my head. Smiling, which was so easy for me to pull off, was suddenly hard to do.

Mother glared at me and grabbed my hand as I gulped down my fourth small cup of wine. "What in the world are you doing" she hissed before taking the wine bottle away from me shaking her head in disappointment.

"Some might think you are upset over his highness getting married."

Watching my two friends get married happily, it made me feel so unlucky. How would you feel if your crush likes someone else and you got rejected 2 times already. Yeah, you would feel pretty hopeless.

Evening approached and mother and father stood up to go in the guest rooms that the royal family had prepared. Hyerin and Prince Yul had already been escorted into their own room to spend their first night together.

I lazily got up feeling the world spin around me. This was the first time I drank any type of alcohol and I was starting to deeply regret it. I tried walking a few steps, stumbling a little, only to be pulled back by a certain someone.

He placed his hand on my back respectfully before helping me balance myself. I turned around and glared at him. My vision was kind of blurry and distorted but I could easily make out who was standing in front of me.

"Kim Yo Han. May I have your permission to badmouth you?"

"Who asks for permission to do that?" He scoffed before turning me back around and walking next to me.

"You're a jerk. A mean jerk. Are you two faced or something? You tell me you don't like me but lead me on by acting all nice." "If you had someone you liked, why didn't you straight up say so earlier" Once the jar finally opened, all the things I wanted to say to him flowed out endlessly.

"You're a betrayer and a liar too. I asked for you to write to me. I asked for you to protect me since I was scared. But you didn't do any of those. You threw me away like I was a piece of rubbish."

My mind felt fuzzy and I couldn't filter what was coming out of my mouth anymore.

Once we got to a certain room, he opened the door for me and I took one of my socks off before balling it up and aiming it at his face.

The way he easily caught it ticked me off even more. Before I could grab my other sock, he came over and dragged me over to the bed.

"You should sleep now, or else you will regret your actions tomorrow morning." I could see a smile threatening to form on his face and I scoffed.

He tucked me into bed before making his way out of the room. I stared at his retreating figure and rubbed my tired eyes.

Before closing the door and leaving, he looked over at me once more.

"I never broke the promise of protecting you, Lady Goeun"

I blinked my eyes trying to process his words before putting the blanket over my head.

"Miss, wake up. We brought you some soup that will help you feel better"

Waking up to a headache is never a good way to start off your day. I got up holding my head as it throbbed in pain. How much did I drink..Picking up the spoon, I was just about to put a spoonful in my mouth before memories from last night flashed by in my mind.

No way I would do such thing... I looked over at my feet in doubt but seeing how I only had one pair on, I gasped in shock. Dropping the spoon, my mouth hung open as I looked at my maids. Confusion was written over their faces as they also stared at my feet.

I don't think I'll be able to look at him in the eye anymore. I have lost all my dignity as a noble woman.

"You didn't allow us to change you into your nightgown last night miss, we deeply apologize for upsetting you." They looked at each other in worry that I would do something to them.

"It's not you guys, It's all on me" I cleared the air between us before slowly getting up.

They had already prepared me a bath and I shooed them all out before washing myself. Getting dressed in a rose gold colored dress, they adorned me in small jewelry before braiding my hair.

We were leaving tonight and I wanted to meet up with Hyerin for a little bit if I can. Seeing her yesterday made me realize how much I missed my friend. Although we wrote letters often, talking to each other is a whole different feeling.

I just hope she didn't see my condition yesterday drinking up all my sorrows. I'm already a bad friend for not feeling happy on her special day.

Just as I was about to get up, an unfamiliar lady came in gracefully before bowing. "We are required to escort you to the place that the crown princess mentioned this morning Lady Goeun"

Following them, I enjoyed the light summer breeze as the sun slowly began to make its way up the sky. The morning hours were quite delightful as the birds chirped melodically.

When we turned the corner, there stood the man I did not want to see at the moment. He was busy talking with the guards holding a serious expression.

I prayed to god for him to not see me as I stood behind the court ladies. How come I see him wherever I go now, but when I lived here for a month or so, he was nowhere to be seen

We passed by him only to be stopped a few steps away. "Is she going to meet the crown prince and princess?, Court lady Eun?"

As the woman nodded, his dark brown eyes bored into mine. "I also had business with his highness so I'll escort her there."

As they all left, I kept quiet as we began to walk. The floor suddenly looked more interesting as I focused on my feet.

"How's your head feeling? I don't think you are able to hold liquor well" he started off the conversation but I still didn't have the courage to face him yet.

"My head is good" short and simple

"How's your parents doing after yesterday's events?" I rolled my eyes hearing him ask that obvious question.

"They're good"

"How's your socks doing?"

"My sock is- wait what?" My face heated up in embarrassment and I looked up at him for the first time today. With a teasing smile, his laugh echoed through the empty hallway.

"Finally, you looked up, Lady Goeun."

"Quit teasing me will you, it was my first time drinking yesterday." During our time, women are not allowed to show even their ankles, let alone their bare feet to men, except for their husbands. Mother always told me to cover up modestly so it still feels like a big deal to me.

I walked away faster and turned left as I heard his voice from afar.

"You're going the wrong way" as if I couldn't be embarrassed enough, I quickly went back and turned right before catching sight of his and her highness's palace building. It was heavily guarded at the front and I waited for Yo Han to come next to me.

As we went inside their bed chamber, I caught sight of them sitting together in front of a big table full of food. This bedroom was very extravagant filled with red and gold decorations and even the beddings were that color.

"Greetings to the crown prince and princess. I am honored to be in the presence of the both of you"

"Goeun, finally" As I bowed to show respect, Hyerin embraced me tightly, catching me off guard.

"Why are you so polite with us Lady Goeun, we are your friends after all" Prince Yul gestured for all of us to sit down and I pointed at Yo Han too.

"Him too?" I whispered to Hyerin and she nodded her head smiling. "Turns out, they're best friends. I saw them hanging out often"

"Oh"

Sitting down awkwardly next to Yo Han, I faced the newly married couple as they were wearing matching white silk clothes.

Hyerin and I catched up to how our lives were these past few months while the other two were discussing something about the patrols in the west area.

Hyerin told me about the agonizing lectures she had to endure but also about her stories with the prince. I smiled as her eyes twinkled with excitement as she blabbered on about her love life.

"How's your life going, anyone new?" She wiggled her eyebrows and I shook my head smiling.

"My parents have been nagging me to get married soon or they'll find someone for me" I pouted and took a sip of my tea.

Yo Han gave a quick glance towards my way but I paid no attention to him. We made a broken deal anyways, what's the point of telling them.

Time passed by as we were engrossed in our own conversations. Once the crown prince's eunuch came in informing him of his schedule, I realized how busy they probably were.

"I'll be taking my leave now. I hope we can see each other later on, maybe at the harvest festival during the autumn?" A knowing smile passed through the both of them.

"We'll try to meet up then, I guess." "Have a safe trip Goeun. It's upsetting to spend such little time with you" she looked sad but I smiled in return.

Once you enter the palace, the little freedom you have will get snatched away from you. She willingly went in and knew all of the burdens that would come with it. However, she looks happy with her husband by her side, so I respect her decision.

"Live a happy life you two, and stay out of harms way." I bowed before turning away from them.

Part 15

The doors opened and I left their room. Feeling a presence behind me, I immediately knew the General had taken his leave as well. If I had known the way back to my guest room, I wouldn't have pathetically stopped and waited for him to lead the way.

"So you're leaving today?" It's unusual how he's the one initiating the conversations now. It was usually the other way around.

"Yes, I'm leaving tonight. I heard in Hyerin's letters that the people who tried to harm his highness got caught. Did you catch them in the act?"

"Yes, there was many people involved, and they either got prisoned or killed based on the degree of their crime. So you don't need to worry anymore"

"I never said I was worried" mumbling, I stayed quiet until we got to my room.

"So this is where we say our farewells, for real now?" Why are we always saying bye to one another..

"Something tells me that this won't be the last time we see each other, Lady Goeun" Before I could ask him why, he was already on his way out of here.

3 weeks passed by and my hopeless romantic self still questioned his words. I spent most of my days painting to improve my skills in art or going for tea in Nari's place.

As I finished my last drawing, my knees were practically begging me to get up and stretch around.

Outside was drizzling lightly, and the sounds of raindrops hitting the roof was very pleasant to hear. I opened my drawer and took out the umbrella brother had personally gotten made for me. It was made out of bamboo and white Hanji paper filled with blue flower designs.

Slipping outside without getting caught by mother or the maids, I felt accomplished as I took a stroll peacefully. The rain cooled down the weather significantly and the sun was hidden behind all the clouds today.

I prepared myself over these few weeks trying to think of a believable story on why I fell out of love with the general. After I drop this news to them, they will certainly ship me off to Lady Byeols house without hesitating.

As I walked down the road, I realized I had gone too far out seeing Lady Byeol's house from a distance. At the entrance, I saw two figures very close to one another, and they were... kissing?!

Closing my innocent eyes, I abruptly turned around, before fastening my steps. Holding the umbrella tightly, I was leaving until a voice stopped me in my tracks.

"HEY! You there!" Realizing that Lady Byeol's son was calling out to me, I mentally facepalmed myself. What was his name again? Racking my brain, I think I heard them say it was Tae Ho.

I turned around to see that the secret woman had left and he was standing there with a furious expression on his face. What did I do? You're the one who got caught. We made eye contact and he strode over realizing who I was.

"What brings you here, my lady? Have you changed your mind about the marriage?" His smirk obvious, he probably thought I went to visit him. "I was taking a nice walk until I saw two people eating each other's faces out."

"I wonder how your mother would act knowing that you've been committing adultery before marriage.. I know for a fact that she would be unhappy with that" I tried to walk away but he kept a tight hold of my arms. My umbrella flew out of my hands and onto the ground, nothing on my head to protect me from the rain now.

"You wouldn't dare" his gaze darkened as he brought his lips dangerously close to my ear. "If we ever do tie the knot, I will make sure to embarrass you and your ridiculously high pride as I bring in many concubines. Your parents love me and my family so don't try acting all tough, Goeunssi, you are on the weaker end."

I struggled against his grip not liking how close he was to me. "Get away from me, you nasty brute. I already said that I have a man in my life, what is wrong with you?!"

"Where is he now? I don't see your hair up indicating that you're taken or a ring on that finger." Tears brimmed in my eyes as I struggled to fight him off. He was starting to scare me and I regretted not taking Areum with me.

"I'd rather stay single forever than build my reputation around you all my life" bitterly speaking, I made sure that he knew I resented him.

Just as I was about to kick his legs, the sound of thundering hooves were heard as a dark brown horse galloped its way towards us. Is that one of our guards? Did they realize that I was gone already?

My heart that was beating fast out of fear was suddenly racing recognizing the man on that horse. As he got off, the grip that Tae ho had on me loosened and I immediately pushed him away from me. Grabbing my umbrella from the ground, I ran over to Yohan's side, knowing that I would always be safe with him.

He analyzed me before noticing my wet clothes and hair. Taking his cloak off, he wrapped me up while I stared at him not believing he was here again. "Excuse me for my actions" Suddenly picking me up by the waist, he mounted me on the horse gently. When I didn't feel the ground under my feet anymore, I held onto his shoulders in fear of falling down.

I've never sat on a horse, or even ridden one in my life, so it was weird being so high up from the ground. I stood as still as a statue waiting for Yohan's instructions.

"Don't even come close to touching her again" I watched as he and Taeho looked at one another with distaste but all I wanted to do was go home and take a warm bath.

"And who are you to her?" My ears perked up as Taeho gritted his teeth in annoyance.

The rain started to pour now and I pulled up my umbrella again, protecting both myself and Yohan's horse.

"Her future husband, and who are you, you sick bastard"

Part 16

My mouth was still gaped open lost for words as Yohan got onto his horse with ease and pulled on the reins. The horse galloped slowly in the rain and I unintentionally leaned into the General, scared that I would fall off. With one hand I held onto his sleeve and with the other, I held the umbrella up for us.

"You know you can put that down, we're already drenched." His warm breath fanned my neck, and I cleared my throat awkwardly.

"Since I have your cloak, I don't want you getting even more wet in the rain. It's the least I could do.."

"He was that man you told me about, wasn't he?" I remembered telling him how I didn't want to marry a pervert back at home.

Scoffing, I held onto his sleeve more tightly. "He's more of a jerk than a pervert, as you can tell. I look at their family with disdain but mother doesn't, since she is very good friends with them."

"By the way, what are you doing here? And why did you tell him that you're my, you know"

"You'll see when you get home." After a while passed, the han's residence came to view.

Once we went inside, Yohan got off first before opening his arms and motioning for me to get down. I slowly held onto him as he carried me down easily.

All the maids came over to us, rushing us to go inside. One of the guards took his horse into the stables nearby.

I went straight to my room to take a warm bath and change into clean clothes. Areum was busy drying my hair and scolding me throughout all this telling me how terrifying it was to see that I disappeared suddenly.

"I didn't think I would be gone for that long" I sheepishly smiled and Areum shook her head before sighing. "You just had to cause trouble when important guests arrived here today miss"

"That's what I am curious about. With what business are they doing here in our place?" Areum looked at me like I had grown two heads or something.

"They're here to ask for your mother and father's blessings regarding the marriage. They wanted to go through with a formal proposal."

I choked on my spit and sprung out of my seat. "He's here for that?! Yohan is??" Pacing around the room, Areum followed close behind with a smile on her face.

"Wow, you really did have a lover huh, you're even calling him by his name casually" "When he heard that you were missing, he was the first to leave and ran out in the rain to find you. We all found that so romantic, even your mother was impressed."

"It's because he's a General, that's his job" I don't know if I was defending him or myself, but I felt the need to explain it.

"let's go then, they're probably waiting for me" Taking a deep breath, I made my way to the dining room, my mouth suddenly drying up out of nervousness. It wasn't my first time meeting his parents but I was nervous to say the least.

There they all were, conversing with another. I heard the men as they discussed the political alliance between the two families and how beneficial it would be for both sides. Mother looked over at me before motioning for me to sit down next to her.

Bowing respectfully, I sat down cautiously, feeling all of their eyes on me. "Forgive me for the immature actions that I displayed today. I hope I didn't cause much trouble or concern to you all"

"None at all my child, the only thing that matters is that you are safe" Yohan's mother gave me her content smile, her eyes slightly crinkling.

Mother was probably fuming inside but since there were guests present, she held it in professionally. The door slid open with a creak, and in came Yo Han with a new attire, his hair put up in a bun and his wavy bangs still a little damp.

He sat down across from me, next to his mother. She looked over at him before lovingly attempting to tuck in a piece of his hair. I thought he would smile at the little gesture but instead he, flinched?"

Clearing his throat, I observed how he looked at her, as if sending her a message through his eyes. The silent exchange was made and she put her hands down on her lap.

"Aww, your son is embarrassed of you taking care of him in front of us." Mother and Father laughed it off, finding it cute.

The mood lightened up as our maids brought in desserts such as dasik (pretty decorative cookies) accompanied by ginger tea.

"Would you be able to give your birthdate, my dear?" Yohan's mother suddenly asked and I nodded my head in understanding. "I'll have it written down and given to you later"

Some mothers like to collect the birthdate of the girl and their sons before taking it to a fortune teller. There, they find out if they are compatible or not, for reassurance.

"While we discuss the marriage date, do you want to show our dear son in law around?" Mother smiled at Yohan as I got up and led the way to my room first.

Once we came in, I made sure we were in the clear before closing the door carefully. "Why are you acting so secretive?" hearing a chuckle behind me, I furrowed my eyebrows.

"This is not the time for jokes, what happened? How did you end up here?" Crossing my arms, I waited for him to explain everything. "I came by horse of course"

"You know that's not what I meant. How did you get into this situation?" All the playfulness gone now, he walked over before sitting down on the ground next to my bed. "There's nothing to complicate, I'm here to get your parents permission and set the date"

I made my way over before sitting down next to him.

"Are you being forced to? If you are then let's go resolve this once and for all. Like you said, marriage is not a joke"

"I'm serious here Lady Goeun, and no, no one forced me, It was solely my decision"

"But what about Hwang Minah? What happened with her?" Seeing him stiffen up, I knew I hit another touchy subject. "I've decided to stop the waiting game here and try to move on with my life"

Something definitely happened. He doesn't look like the type to move on that fast. "So are you using me General, to get over her?"

"You can take it that way, however , I, thought that you would be the perfect person to help me."

Leaning closer to me, I watched as his eyes scanned my face, looking for any reactions. "Help me so that at the end, you are the only one that occupies this stubborn heart of mine" Flustered, my heart skipped a beat and my cheeks turned a little rosy.

"I think I know why you chose me, dear general." Now it was his turn to be confused.

"Once you feel an attraction towards someone, falling for them will be much easier and less time consuming."

Seeing his ears turn a light shade of red, I let out a hearty laugh, enjoying the fact that I made the man in front of me flustered with just a few words.

Areum suddenly came in with a tray filled with many kinds of freshly cut up fruits. Seeing us so close to one another, she closed her eyes out of embarrassment. "I-I'll just put these here on the ground. You can eat them if you like o-or just leave them and I'll pick it up later" she rushed out quickly and I laughed at her cuteness.

"She's only sixteen, so she tends to be dramatic sometimes." I picked up the tray before going back to where we were sitting.

"Now, where were we at?" Taking a slice of the apple, I handed him a piece before grabbing one for myself. "Shall we discuss our terms? I'm sure you also have some things you want from me"

He thought about it before shaking his head. "I don't have anything else to add. How about you?" I thought he would have a list of things he would expect from me but I guess I was wrong.

"I have two conditions."

"As long as this marriage is valid, I would prefer that you don't get any concubines." Many men, especially the royal family has multiple women left and right, so I was worried for Hyerin when she first became the crown princess. Hopefully, Prince Yul will go against all odds and change history as a king who only had one wife.

"Okay, what's the second?"

"Let me take one of my maids with me once we get married. Will you permit that?" He nodded his head before teasingly saying "I thought you would ask me to give you buckets of gold for your Dowry. I was worried for nothing"

I rolled my eyes before shoving a grape in his mouth. "I'm not that hard to please, so don't feel too burdened."

Our evening passed by like that and Yohan went in a spare room to sleep. His family was staying the night due to the bad weather conditions.

When I was getting ready to sleep, mother suddenly came in with a bright smile on her face. Wasn't she supposed to be mad? "My baby, you're now getting married soon" she took me in her embrace and I awkwardly hugged her back.

"I had my suspicions when you said you already had someone but today is the happiest I've felt in a long time." She stroked my hair and I let her do so, liking the fact that I made my mother proud.

"We set the date to the end of this month so we have plenty of time to prepare your clothes and all of that." Once she let go, I looked at her before sighing.

"What about older brother? I don't think he will attend the wedding if he doesn't come home this month." Mother's face turned sullen and I felt bad for bringing it up when she was just in a good mood.

"If he comes, we'll welcome him with open arms but if he doesn't, then... it's all on him"

Mother left to her room and I made my way to my covers, sleep taking over me instantly.

"I hope we weren't too much of a hinderance to you all by staying over the night." Yohan's mother stood at the entrance with her family, their horses and palanquins ready to depart.

"Oh no, it was a pleasure meeting you all again. I had such a wonderful time yesterday" I watched as the two women talked with each other as if they were long-term friends that go way back.

I eyed Yohan, seeing him wear the gat (traditional korean hat), making him look a little different. Noticing me openly staring at him, he walked over before looking down at my hands. I looked down too, trying to see what might be wrong with my hands.

"My cloak?" With his eyebrows arched, he stared at me as I tried to think of what he was talking about.

"Your cloak?... Oh! Your cloak!" Just remembering about it, I was about to call for someone to fetch them but he shook his head no. "You can give them to me the next time we meet."

"Or you can just keep it, my lady"

Part 17

Time whizzed by, me and mother got closer in a span of a month spending time together. We went to the market together to select fabrics and picked out things that would go well for my future husband's side of the family.

Learning that Yohan has a younger sister was a little surprising because he just gave off an only child aura. She is only eight years old, that is why they didn't bring her, afraid that she might not be able to handle the trip.

I sent out a letter to Hyerin about my marriage with Yohan and she apparently freaked when she read it. I got a reply back the next day, her letter a little messy seeing her rushed handwriting due to excitement.

She exclaimed saying how happy she was about the news but was shocked on who I was marrying. She said that the crown prince laughed it off before saying that he called it, making her more puzzled.

Sadly she isn't able to attend, but she sent me a gift yesterday. Once I opened it up, a beautiful chest with painting tools inside came to view. I was touched seeing how she still remembered what things I loved to do.

About a week ago, gifts from his side of the family came in a big carriage and we sent ours back to them in exchange. Sending out invitations was also a hard task, as me and mother pondered over who to give it out to.

We even hosted a tea party a few days before the wedding ceremony, and I purposely invited Lady Byeol just to see her reaction. Everything went smoothly and it was finally the big day everyone was waiting for.

I barely got enough sleep before Areum woke me up very early complaining how we were late already. "Areumah, we don't have to rush so much. A wedding won't start without its bride anyways."

"They can wait a little bit" I yawned and sat up stretching.

"We need to get you dressed, put your makeup on, and do your hair beautifully." Your mother is up and dressed already, she'll scold you if she sees you like this"

I washed up before sitting down as 3 of my maids dressed me in layers of silk clothing and did my hair. I wore a red dress that had blue, yellow, and long white stripes on the sleeves. I couldn't see my hands anymore because the white part of the sleeve was intentionally made long to help with the bowing process. They put my hair in a low braided bun before putting the hair accessories and headpiece on top. Then they put the bridal ribbon on each side of my hair pin.

Wearing my hanbok shoes and getting my makeup done was the last part before my stomach rumbled in hunger. "Areum let's go eat something, I am starving" Whining, I sulked until they gave me grapes to munch on.

Once everything was done, I got up with the help of my maids and slowly made my way out to the grand back yard. Ribbons were decorated everywhere and the table laden was at the very center, covered with a blue cloth on one side and red on the other.

The candles were put on each side, dishes filled the table as I also saw a pair of gourd halves. A rooster and hen was also wrapped up in silk, and everyone was at the sidelines, watching everything unfold.

Cushions and a smaller table were put on each side with wash bins next to them. "Keep your head down miss" I tried listening to them while the two assisted me to my spot. However, taking a small peak, I saw Yohan as he was standing on the opposite side of me wearing a dark blue colored traditional robe. We had to both stay serious during the ceremony or it was said that it brings shame to your family and yourself.

The ceremony started as we cleansed our hands. The wedding officiant told us how many times we had to bow and what each of them represented in our marriage. We formally bowed to one another multiple times before finally sitting down. I thought my head piece would fall off halfway through but I managed.

They filled the gourds with wine before placing it to our lips. I took a sip before the gourds were exchanged from each side. Drinking from his gourd, I felt a little shy, but got it done as well.

"You may now eat the dates and the jujube" Eating the stuff given to me, I tried to see what Yohan was doing but the laden table was too tall, blocking my view. Hearing the joyful chatters around me, I saw how everyone was enjoying themselves, making me feel content.

"Now, bow once to your parents"

Mother had tears in her eyes while father looked proud of us. Older brother didn't come home this month, missing out on his one and only sister's special day. Should I also do that on his wedding day?

"And now bow once to the guests present today"

The ceremony was concluded as they brought me to the palanquin. Saying our farewells, Yo Han got on his horse easily while I struggled to fit my dress inside. Mother and father asked for the food they prepared to be put in a small carriage, a little gift for my in laws.

They told me last night that Areum would be sent to me in a few days, since she had to finish up things here. The ride was long and tiring, but whenever I tried to sleep, my hair accessories kept poking my head and neck.

Once it came to a stop, Yo Han was the one to open it before holding out his hand. "You look worn out" I don't know if he was teasing or worrying about me, but I took his hand and got out, fixing my dress so it looks presentable.

Yo han's mother and father came over to us and I brought them the food mother had packed for them. We did our bows again and they followed their traditions as well. We did the chestnut and date toss which everyone enjoyed.

The new maids here escorted me to our room and I sent them out before awkwardly sitting on the bed, not knowing what to do. After a while passed, I started looking through the drawer that seemed to have my stuff inside, and found my mirror before starting to take out all the accessories and jewelry. Neatly putting everything away, my hair was now in a simple long braid.

Mother had kicked father out of the room last night stating that she had something really important to tell me. Once we both sat down, she explained to me how your first night is supposed to go and I stopped her halfway, feeling my face go completely red. Talking with your mother about these topics is way more embarrassing so I didn't know how to act.

Would Yohan and I do..that..?

Fanning my face, I called in one of the girls that were behind my door. "Could you bring in some meals for me and..my husband" she nodded before heading back to their kitchen.

When am I going to be able to get into comfortable clothes? Although it was made of fine silk, I felt like I was wrapped up in layers of blankets on a hot summer day.

Fanning myself with the end of my dress, I scanned the room seeing how it was pretty spacious. It is a little empty but it will surely change soon once I add a few things here and there. There was also a separate door on the left which I assumed to be the dressing room.

"You know you can go and change, the dressing room won't open its doors for you" startled by his voice, I turned to see Yohan leaning against the door with a teasing look. The room was lit with a few candles, and the room was dead silent a minute ago.

"Atleast make a sound when you enter, I almost blurted out some indecent words." My heart had yet to calm down as I felt it beating loudly in my chest.

He came over and sat across from me and soon enough, the woman from earlier came in with our food. The aroma was enough to make me realize how hungry I was, just relying on the grapes and dates I ate today didn't help my energy levels.

Waiting for him to pick up his chopsticks first was torture as he took his time scanning the food before looking at his own attire.

"Shall we change first before eating?" My eyes felt like they twitched for a moment as I stared at him dumbfounded.

He's trying to get on my nerves and we haven't even been married for a whole day yet.

Seeing me agitated, he picked up his utensils rather quickly before grabbing a piece of meat. "Here" he held it up for me to eat and I pointed at myself confused.

"You're supposed to eat first though"

"I want my wife to be treated as an equal and not someone below her husband" I felt myself go shy from his words as that was something that can't be easily said or done.

"I'm sorry to ruin this sweet moment but I'm not very fond of meat. I like fish or chicken though"

Blinking innocently, I kept my mouth open as he picked something else before feeding it to me.

"Point taken"

Part 18

Nervous

    That was the feeling I was having as I changed into my nightgown. It was late into the night and Yohan had already washed and changed before me. Contemplating on what I would do or say, I finally mustered up my courage to come out and face this head on like a mature woman.

Stepping out, I was just about to speak until I saw Yohan dozed off on the bed. I scoffed and mentally face palmed myself before walking my way towards him. What was all that worrying for Goeun

Carefully taking off his socks, I put the covers over him before laying down as well. His hair was put down and I admired the small wavy locks sweeping over his eyes.

The sound of his slow breathing was heard as he slept peacefully, and I scooted just a little closer to him. He must've been really tired from traveling back and forth from my residence to his place.

Soon enough, my eyelids felt heavy and I too, fell into a deep slumber, fatigue taking over my body.

Waking up early for the day, I forced my body to get up before picking out something to wear. The maids here are a bit on the older side and it's hard for me to converse with them, so I decided from today that I will get ready on my own. Atleast until Areum comes in a few days to help me with my hair.

Wearing a sage green dress, I put my hair up before going over to Yohan's side. He was still sound asleep and I smiled to myself, knowing that this man is now my husband.

I gently patted his shoulder until he stirred awake, his eyes adjusting to the brightness. "You're up quite early"

I was startled hearing his deep raspy morning voice, but it sounded quite nice. It wouldn't be too bad hearing this every morning.

"I just wanted to make a good first impression to your family. I don't think they would like me sleeping in from the first day" As he got up and stretched around, I handed him his socks and he stared at me suspiciously.

"You didn't do anything bad to me yesterday, did you?" I smiled in annoyance before pretending to think about last night. "I think we were supposed to do something, but we went against the customs last night"

"Were you unhappy?" "Then should we do it now?"

"No!" Flustered, I threw a pillow at him which he caught easily.

"Then I think compared to other people, our case is a bit special. And I have yet to be intimate with you, lady Goeun" All jokes aside, I suddenly remembered why he got married in the first place.

I guess the excitement of getting married got to me because I totally forgot about Hwang Minah and his complicated feelings towards her.

Nodding my head, I realized how foolish I was acting, not considering his side of the story. Although I married him because I fell for him, he married me to try and get rid of that affection and fondness he has towards someone else.

"But that doesn't mean I will neglect you or not care for you. You are my wife and my forever partner"

As he got himself ready, I went out to the dining area to see if anyone was awake. All the workers were busy doing their own things and the table was slowly getting filled with dishes of food.

"It's good to see you up and awake, dear" Yohan's mother, or I mean my mother in law, came out elegantly with her daughter next to her.

She was quite shy hiding behind her mom and a smile went on my face unknowingly. "Did you guys have a good nights sleep?"

As we all sat down, I tried to start a conversation with the young girl but she didn't seem to want to talk with me.

"I named her Nari because I wanted my daughter to grow up and bloom beautifully like a lily"

"That's a very beautiful meaning, I also have a friend with the same name as yours" Nari hid herself even more noticing that we were talking about her more than usual.

Yohan came in and sat down next to me, without greeting his mom or saying hi to his younger sister. I nudged him lightly but he ignored me completely leaving me confused. Everyone was quiet all of a sudden and it felt as if the air became chillier.

Once we finished breakfast, Yohan's parents gave us permission to go out and have fun for the day, and I was determined to confront him on his behavior.

As we were walking along the road, I put my arms around his before asking "why were you so cold with your family today? Did you perhaps have a fight?"

"I- am not very close with them" he smoothly avoided my question but I decided to let him off the hook this time. "Is it because you don't come home often? I heard from your mother that you're busy at the palace almost everyday"

He nodded his head before looking down at me thoughtfully. "I'm given a few more days off of my work duties, but afterwards, I'll be at the palace most of the time. Will you be okay waiting for me?"

"I think I already knew the consequences when I decided to marry a General. A responsible one at that" His eyes softened and I let out a little laugh.

"And the palace is close to our home so I expect you to come home occasionally. Or else I will barge in your workplace unannounced. You see, I also have connections" knowing that I was referring to Prince Yul and Hyerin, he patted my head before shaking his head smiling.

"That, would be a scary sight"

Our free days passed by like that, us enjoying each others presence and me trying to get closer to his younger sister.

As I laid down in bed, Yohan was busy getting things ready for tomorrow, since he was leaving to the palace. It was raining again outside, the sound of low thunder rumbling every few minutes.

Seeing his sword and clothes, a question popped up in my head.

"What made you want to become a General? Why not a scholar, minister, or maybe even a merchant?" He paused what he was doing before turning towards me.

"At first I wanted to make my father proud of me." Humming, I encouraged him to continue.

"Then, my purpose changed as I felt the need to have the ability and power to protect the people most closest to me."

"So.. are you happy with your choice?" I patted the spot next to me and he dropped what he was doing before coming over.

"I'm not sure yet" Laying down a little farther away from me, we stared at each other absentmindedly. "By the way, how are you so good at shooting arrows? I saw you a while back in the palace"

With a smile he told me a few snippets from his childhood, from the days he picked up a sword or practiced his martial arts. "I used to practice from a young age, and knowing how to shoot arrows felt like the coolest thing to do back when I was a kid"

"It's still cool though. Atleast for me" Adding my own comments into his story, I imagined a little Yohan running around this household, making me giggle.

"Practicing archery on my own was a bit hard so I had Minah to accompany me. We used to do everything together, whether it was going to the market, having a sword match, riding horses,........"

As he talked on and on about Minah, I realized how much he misses those times they spent together. She must've been his everything as they grew up next to one another.

"How long have you known each other?" As he heard my voice, it's like a ghost that was possessing him came out as he finally realized what he was talking about.

He avoided eye contact and cleared his throat awkwardly. "We met when we were both nine years old. Then we parted once I turned eightteen."

I can't believe I'm talking about my husbands love life with another girl. Well.. I signed up for this

I got into a sitting position and was just about to ask about what happened to her until he cut me off completely.

Pulling me back down, he put the covers over us before blowing out the candles. "I'm trying to forget about that woman so remembering all the times with her won't help me at all"

"But in order to overcome it, the first step is to accept it"

"Accept what?" His voice a little softer, I realized how much he was hanging on to my every word.

"Accept what that love meant to you. Then, you find ways to reconnect with yourself again. Over those years, you probably already went through a lot, either blaming her or yourself. I don't know what happened between you two but you, Yohan, is still confined in the past."

"Have you ever reached out to your friends or family for help before?" Seeing him shake his head no, I let out a sigh before opening my arms.

"It's dark and it's raining outside, so you can let it all out, I won't hear or see a thing" he looked at me for a second as if hesitating on whether to do it or not. He's like a little kid sometimes

"I think your silence means a yes. But if you don't feel comfortable doing this, you can tell me anytime"

I scooted closer to him before wrapping my arms around him, gently patting his back. He didn't seem to be emotional but I felt him relax into my touch. With the soft sound of the rain hitting the roof and the warmness engulfing me, my heart and mind felt at peace. Soon enough, sleep knocked on my door and I drifted off into my dreamland.

Part 19

Once Yohan had left, Areum came to the Kim residence later in the day, carrying a bag with all her things inside. "Miss Goeun! I'm finally here!" Although I was really glad seeing her again, her mouth wouldn't stop running the moment she came in through that door.

"Areum-ah, my head is about to explode. How did you gather all these news in just one week? So many things happened in a short amount of time compared to when I actually lived there." Shrugging her shoulders, she made her way inside bowing to everyone and introducing herself enthusiastically.

Another two weeks passed as I patiently waited for Yohan to return home to me. I told him I can wait but how could he not visit me or his family briefly before leaving again?

Hyerin wrote to me saying that Prince Yul apologized in advance since he feels responsible for ruining our first month of marriage. Yohan had work piled up from before and after the wedding, so he was really busy right now. Another problem had arisen in Hanyang, so he was also put in charge of it.

Fine. I'll just wait one more week.. With that thought, I stepped into Nari's room watching the little girl playing with her handmade dolls. She looked just like her father, with her black hair but her face features resembled her mother. "Nari-ah, mother gave us permission to go out to have fun today. Wanna join me?"

As she silently nodded her head, I showed her what I was hiding behind my back and her eyes lit up in excitement. "Although not many people do kite flying in this season, I thought it would be fun since it's windy today."

As I led her outside and into the palanquin, mother came out with a few blankets and a guard behind her. "Nari gets sick easily so come back before the evening. She doesn't go outside often. I also packed her dolls and a pair of shoes just in case" Nodding my head, I took all the stuff from her hands before getting in myself.

The 4 other workers carried the palanquin easily, pulling it up in one go.

"Nari, do you have any friends that can join us? We can bring them if you would like" Looking out the small window, she shook her head before holding onto her kite tightly.

"It's okay then, we'll just have fun on our own" holding her tiny hand, I made sure she felt reassured with me. We went out into a nearby town that had open fields and a place to eat delicious food close by.

We walked a little farther away from where the palanquin was at so we could run to get the kites going.

As the hours passed by us goofing around and flying the kites, Nari's stomach rumbling stopped me in my tracks.

Turning around to the young male guard, looking no older than eighteen, I pointed at the direction of the diner not far from here. "Would you be able to get some food and drinks that Nari would like and set it up with the blankets here. I don't want her to get hungry or cold once she's done playing."

"Of course my lady" as he hurried off, I took a quick glance at what Nari was doing before walking over to the palanquin to get all the stuff my mother in law packed.

Once I grabbed everything I needed, I started to head back until I noticed that something was very wrong. The field felt too empty... and very quiet.

"Nari? Where are you?" A dreaded feeling crept inside of me as I looked around for Nari as she was nowhere to be seen. She was just running around a few moments ago..

Turning my head frantically, I dropped the stuff in my hands realizing that both Nari and her kite was gone. Looking around the field surrounded by the tall grass and wheat, panic started to rise within me as I hurriedly ran to every corner of the place, calling out her name.

"NARI-AH" Tears welling up my eyes, all the different things that might've happened to her ran across my mind, my heart hammering in my chest.

Where could she be?! She barely talks so if she's lost she won't let out a single peep. "If you can hear my voice Nari, let out the biggest scream you can muster up, I will find you, okay?" The utter silence continued on as I urged for her to call out to me, my voice betraying me as I was on the verge of breaking down.

Seeing a familiar figure running my way with the things in his hands, I finally let out a sob, not knowing how to control the emotions coursing through me.

"My lady why are you crying? Where's.. Young Miss?" Looking around, the color drained from his face as he also started searching in panic, knowing that if she isn't found, mother will have both of our heads. His will be gone first. Then those innocent workers that have no clue on what's happening, and then finally me.

We both ran into the nearby bustling town that was filled with many people. "Have you seen a girl about this height with black hair wearing a white and yellow dress?"

Asking everyone around me, they simply shrugged off my pleas as they carried on with their lives. Some looked at us with sympathy while others shook their heads no in annoyance.

"Miss, I think we should go back and report this to the household. With many more people and guards, we have more of a chance of finding her"

My eyes casted upon a stable with many horses and I brought out my pouch filled with money inside.

"You go by horse, I'll stay here and try to find her with the help of those 4 workers" bowing his head, he immediately left and I continued on with my search.

Knocking on each house gate and each market store, the night stretched on as it felt like I was running around in circles.

Going back to the field area, I searched through the tall grass and ventured beyond noticing a faint light that grabbed my attention. The place was covered by trees and bushes, but it still looked like a house that is being used.

The self guilt was killing me as I blamed myself over and over again for not being more attentive with her. If she isn't found after this, I don't think I'll ever go back to how I was before.

Noticing a familiar kite stuck in the tree branches nearby, a glimmer of hope rose in me as I ran in the direction of that house.

"Is anyone in there?!" Knocking on the door, I tried to sound half sane so they won't be too scared to open it for me.

"Who- are you? What business do you have in my quiet residence?" An old woman, looking to be in her fifties, came out with a frown etched on her face.

"Did a girl, about this height, with black hair, come running in this direction? She has a white and yellow dress on and I saw her kite stuck on a tree nearby"

"How do I know that you are a safe person for her to be around?"

"She's here right? Please, I'm her sister, I'm sure she will recognize me if you let me in" The old woman stared at me suspiciously before calling out to someone.

"Dear, I think someone you know has come for you. Would you come here for a second" Just as I had hoped, a sleepy looking Nari came out rubbing her tired eyes. Noticing my presence, she quickly ran over before holding on to my dress, with tears flowing down rapidly.

Hugging her tiny body, I took her into my embrace as I sighed in relief. The woman stared at us shaking her head in disapproval. "I think I built my house in a wrong location. I moved here to live a secluded life but always have random strangers coming over. What a nuisance.."

Wiping my tears away, I held the woman's hands out of gratitude before bowing a few times. "Thank you for taking care of Nari until I came. I can't thank you enough for this, would you like anything as a repayment?"

"Repay me with money the next time we meet. You both look like you come from a well payed off family"

As we left her place, I carried little Nari on my back as she was really sleepy. "Why did you wonder off so suddenly like that, everyone was very worried about you" scolding her for a little bit, I walked under the moonlight as the winds started to pick up a little faster.

"I think I left your dolls and blankets in the field, are you okay with that? Don't worry though, I'll get you an even better one later" I think I was talking all to myself because I heard no response from Nari as she slept, her arms wrapped around my neck loosely.

Noticing many guards, horses, and a few palanquins, I just knew I was going to be in big trouble by her mother and father. Walking up to them, they immediately took Nari off of me before wrapping her with a blanket.

The next thing they did totally caught me off guard as something powerful struck my cheek with a hard slap, leaving me too stunned to speak. "I don't know how I even trusted you with my precious girl. You all won't be alive if I see even a scratch on my daughter."

Mother in laws face was a chilling sight as her eyes were lit in fury. I held my cheek with my hand as a single tear streamed down my face. "I cherish her as much as you do, and I understand you're angry with me, but don't stoop so low as to lash out on me"

"Why you-" "that's enough." father in law's stern voice shut the both of us up as he escorted her away, and everyone began to depart home.

As I stared at the ground, my money pouch got placed in my hands. "I understand if you don't want to come home for tonight." The young guard from earlier gave me a sad smile, the guilt again bubbling up inside me.

"The highest punishment I can get is probably getting my position taken away from me so don't worry. I'm glad you found young miss on time"

"Could I ask for one more favor before you leave?" As he nodded his head, I gave him a few coins before saying..

"Please..call my husband here. I'll be staying at an inn for tonight"

Part 20

"Please bring a warm meal inside my room for tonight" paying her extra, she smiled at the coins before leading the way to a spare room. "Right away young lady"

Closing the door to my room, I finally sat down, the aching in my legs reminding me of the earlier events.

Aish, this is so unfair. I ran around the whole night to find her daughter and then I get slapped in return. I don't know which part of my body I should complain about first. My stomach is begging for food, my legs are killing me, my back hurts, my cheeks are stinging, but my heart aches the most.

"Young miss, here's your food" sliding the tray inside, I silently thanked her before beginning to satisfy my hunger.

It was way past midnight when I was jolted awake by the knockings on the door. I don't even deserve sleep do I?

"Whoever you are, get lost, I am done being nice and patient for today"

"Be nice one more time and open the door for your husband"

"My husband isn't here.." Processing those words after a minute or two, my eyes snapped open in realization. All sleepiness gone now, I hurriedly opened it to see the one person that I truly needed at this moment.

My lower lip naturally quivered into a pout and before I knew it, the tears began falling one by one, startling poor Yohan along the way.

Closing the door behind us, he started to wipe my tear stained cheeks with his sleeves, lowering his body so we were at the same level. "Do you want to tell me who made you cry like this or would you like a hug first?"

"Both"

Wrapping his arms around me, he pulled me in by the waist, his other hand on the back of my head. Stroking my hair, he managed to calm me down after a while, my breathing slowly regulating back to normal. Being embraced when you are at your lowest seems to work wonders as I felt both understood and protected.

"N-Nari got lost while we were flying kites and I searched for her all evening. I felt both scared and responsible for losing sight of her for a bit, and the guilt was crushing me inside."

"Why are you so hard on yourself? She got lost on her own and you found her at the end. You did the most you could do on your end, so all you deserve is praise and commendation"

"Look, I got a few scratches on my ankle" showing him my small injuries, the feeing of being cared for was really nice.

"Where else?" "My back hurts too" gently rubbing my back in a circular motion, he continued with my pampering.

"What else?" "My cheek still has a dull pain" His hold on me got firmer, as if telling me that I'll be alright from now on.

"Let's go to bed now, we both look like we need some rest"

After eating our morning meal, we headed out and I stared at the four legged creature in front of me with a straight face. I admire this horse but it will make me feel queasy if I ride on it right after eating.

While Yohan paid for the meal, I attempted to get on the horse alone. Everyone makes it look so easy but why won't my darn leg get the hang of it?!

I guess I'll learn next time.. Stroking this dark haired beauty, I opened my palms in front of him revealing a sugar cube.

"Look what I got youu, but in exchange, don't tell your owner about my failed attempts. It's a secret between us"

"What are you whispering about over there?" Yohan came over wearing a questionable look and I laughed it off before motioning at his horse. "Does he have a name?"

"A horse is a horse, I don't really talk to it much." He mouthed a what after I gave him a judge-mental look. "You're going to hurt his feelings, he's been carrying you around throughout all your journeys." "Let's name him Kkum (dream)" (pronounced as koom) . It sound fun to say, kkum kkumah"

"Dream on, my lady. Now, shall we go back?"

"Do you have to leave now? Can't you come in with me?" I watched as he got on his horse again, ready to leave. "I had some unfinished business left to do. I'll be back soon" He looked apologetic as he ran his hands through his hair not knowing what to say.

"Three times"

He halted in confusion, waiting for me to go on. "Come home to me three times a week" "make it a promise" before he could refuse, I quickly made my way inside, ignoring his poor attempts on stopping me.

Looking through the house, the place somehow felt empty, even though the maids and workers were tending to the chores as usual. As I made my way to my room, Areum came running to me with tears in her eyes.

"Miss Goeun!" Hugging me tightly, she scanned me from head to toe before sighing in relief. "I thought something bad happened to you. The guard told me you were alright but I didn't believe him and demanded to know where you were."

"I slept in a warm place and was served delicious food. You didn't have to worry about me"

"By the way, where's everyone else?" By everyone, I meant Nari and mother in law

"They went to a physician nearby to get a checkup on young miss, just in case"

Humming in response, I looked at my clothes seeing how it was a bit dirty and wrinkled up. "I need to take care of myself now. Go prepare a bath for me Areum, I feel grimy"

Once mother came back, she ignored my presence completely but Nari gave me a small wave with a smile on her face. There's no need for me to feel shame in my actions, I did nothing wrong.

Holding my chin up, I smiled back before walking away with pride.

Part 21

"What are you so busy with lately, my dear husband? Don't lie to me, Hyerin told me that you guys already finished your task a while ago."

"Are you done talking to the door miss?" Areum looked at me disapprovingly as I stared at the pretty white door in front of me. It's been a while since that incident and everything has quieted down. I'm still on mother's bad side but I can't do anything about that anymore.

"Yeah, I'm done. I will confront him today when he comes home"

With a determined look, I was going to wait at the entrance until I saw a big carriage in front of the gate. It was empty but I wondered why it was in front of our place. "Who-??"

Workers came rushing in with Yohan behind them, a mischievous smile on his face. Pointing at the people grabbing our stuff and furniture, I was dumbfounded. "What-?"

Mother and Father in law came rushing out because of the commotion clearly confused by what's happening. "What in the world are you guys doing?!"

Yohan strode over to me before clasping our hands together. "We decided to move out and live separately from today. The preparations have already been made so I hope you both understand"

I was just baffled trying to understand when we even decided on that together. "When-" Quietly whispering to Yohan, I asked "When did we decide on this again?"

"Just now, so go pack your things Goeun, and bring whoever you want along to our new home"

And that is how I ended up bringing Areum and that young guard along with me. They stood happily with their stuff in their hands while I rechecked if we got everything in the carriage.

"We'll be going now mother and father. I'll visit often to play with Nari and we can chat over tea sometime." Bowing my head, I avoided eye contact since they seemed mad at this sudden situation. Don't blame me, I am just going with the flow as well.

"You are officially crazy, Yohanssi" Our new residence was very close to the palace and it looked very new, as if it was renovated recently. A beautiful garden was at the front and even the back yard was spacious. If the outside is this pretty, I want to see how the inside looks like. "Were we that rich that you bought a new property?"

"Did you think your husband was dirt poor?" He chuckled before leading us inside, looking over at me every few seconds, waiting for my reaction.

"Will I be able to recruit more people to work here? If not, then that's totally fine, I'm sure I can manage" I checked our bedroom before going into the kitchen with a big smile on my face.

"Did you know that your wife is an excellent cook? What would you like for dinner?" He laughed silently at my excitement on the different kinds of pots and fresh ingredients this place was already furnished with.

"Aren't you going to ask me why we moved or how I got all this done in a short amount of time?"

"Okay then, let's start with that first. Why did we suddenly leave like that? It's quite unheard of, moving out of your in-laws house this early in marriage"

"I wanted you to feel comfortable and safe , not worrying about what that wo- mother is going to say or her horrible mood swings. I hate seeing my wife be treated with disrespect"

My stomach did a few turns and backflips in there as I gained yet again, more respect for this man in front of me.

"How shall I ever repay you, as you have bestowed such a grand gift to me" exaggerating my words, I managed to bring back the cheerful mood we had going on.

"Repay me by taking good care of this place as the lady of the house."

Nodding my head, we spent the rest of the day touring around the place and moving everything in, just the way I liked it. As I finished cooking with Areum, she held out two bottles of Makgeolli (rice wine) excitedly.

"You are way too young to drink these things, give that to me" we fought over them as she ran around the kitchen, holding the wine safely. "I'll drink only a sip Lady Goeun. And plus, it would be nice to drink after a hard days work!"

Sighing in defeat, I shooed her out before grabbing the tray of food and heading out to the balcony. As I carefully placed it on the table, Yohan poured the drinks for us before sitting down.

Areum had a bottle in her hand as I pulled her aside, quietly talking in a hushed voice "You and that guard can eat in the dining room inside. And please, don't drink too much, I don't know what kind of a drunk you are"

"I love you my lady" This girl is getting cheekier everyday. I scoffed before pushing her out playfully.

Outside was very beautiful as I gazed out at the stars, scattered out in the sky. Eating here while enjoying the peaceful night was definitely a good idea.

"How well can you hold your liquor?" Clinking the bowls together, I took a sip remembering that I'm a lightweight drinker.

"Hmm, I can handle maybe two to three bottles?"

"Oh no, then I should bring atleast 3 more bottles over here." as I pretended to get up, he threw his head back in laughter. "Are you perhaps trying to get me drunk?"

"Maybe?"

As I placed some of the pajeon (korean pancake) on his rice bowl, he lifted an eyebrow in surprise. "Do you want to ask me something? You're acting suspiciously.."

"I am curious about something, but I think it would be hard for you to answer right away" biting the inside of my cheek out of nervousness, I didn't know how to bring it up as it has been lingering in my mind lately.

"Go ahead then" ....."The people back at home... aren't your real family, are they?.."

The tension was suffocating as we both sat in silence, until Yohan placed the bottle on his end of the table.

"I think you should get a few more of these before we start"

Part 22

"The man you know is my biological father, so don't jump to wild conclusions just yet" The idea that he was maybe adopted flew out of my head instantly.

"My father was forced into an arranged marriage with my mother, which isn't anything new. Love gradually formed in their relationship and after a few years, I was born."

I listened as he hesitated to continue, wiping his hands on his lap every few seconds. "My mother.......my poor mother, she fell ill once I turned eight years old." Knowing where this was now heading, my heart ached as he continued with pain evident in his eyes. As if he was back in that time again, reliving those memories.

"She slowly got worse, her muscles giving up on her as she laid bedridden for the next few years. Her beautiful complexion turning pale and her lips losing color, I regret the fact that I can't remember her well sometimes. If I had known she would pass away so early, maybe I wouldn't have gone out to play and would've sat by her side."

"At just twelve years old, I lost my safe haven, my protector, my selfless and warmhearted mother" As he drank his second bottle of wine, I held his arm, urging him to stop. "Let's leave it for another time, hm?"

He shook his head before releasing my hand, and started to laugh bitterly, wiping away the tears that were clouding his eyes. "One year had barely passed when that father of mine married another woman"

That would explains all the times they treated each other coldly and why he doesn't come home often. I believe I'm pretty good at comforting people but in this situation, I didn't know whether to insult his father or his step mother, or just not mention anything at all.

"No child should ever go through that, carrying such a heavy burden on their small shoulders""Despite that, you grew up to be a fine man. Many people regard you as one of the best protectors of the land, a loyal man who takes his job seriously.." trying to distract him from the topic, I slowly began taking away the wine that he was chugging down, seeing how he was starting to get tipsy.

"Maybe your father couldn't bear the loneliness any longer and also wanted you to have a motherly figure in your life again. Although it didn't work out, he probably had a good intention when he made that decision. You did say they loved each other very much.."

"Bullshit" My eyes widened in surprise hearing him curse for the first time,

"Do you think I would marry someone else if something ever happened to you?"

".....no? I don't think so, would you?"

"Then there's your answer" He laid down on the ground before gazing up at the sky above us. As I waddled my way next to him, in a hushed voice, I heard him say "Mother.....are you proud of me?"

"I think you need to speak louder than that. Your mother's soul is pretty high up, watching you from beside those stars" He brought his hand up, as if wanting to reach the sky, before saying in a louder voice "Mom, I miss you" ....Both of our tears never came as the bittersweet moment passed along. Feeling a lump in my throat, I looked over at Yohan who had closed his eyes moments ago. His face was a little flushed from the aftereffects of the wine.

Looking up at the sky again, I made a silent promise to myself. I'll be his safe haven from now on mother, you can be rest assured and relax peacefully up there..

Autumn made its way into the world as the leaves on the trees became bright orange, mixed with the hue of yellow and red.

I brought in a few more workers to help run the house since me and Areum can't handle everything on our own. While they put up the lanterns for the harvest festival coming up, I was busy arranging some flowers for our trip later.

Yohan started to come home everyday after we moved so we have gotten a lot closer now. He trusts me and is comfortable with me, but I don't know if he likes me in a romantic way yet. I know for a fact that he already has me wrapped around his finger though.

"What are you thinking about so deeply?" Grabbing a flower from my hand, he placed it behind my ear as I looked up at him. "Nothing much..are you ready to go?"

I grabbed the flowers and he picked up the basket with clean towels next to me. "You're wearing something new today" he scanned my appearance and I smiled in appreciation. I had worn my new beige dress with matching shoes specifically for today's trip.

"I want to make a good first impression"

It took a while to reach our destination, the place we arrived at was a vast place with a few hills and trees. As I followed Yohan up one of the hills, I tried to not get my dress dirty and not fall backwards at the same time.

"Here we are" Yohan placed the basket down next to the stone that had the name Kim Yeona on it. I slowly made my way and placed the flowers down as Yohan wiped the dust off of the stone and brushed off the leaves.

"How have you been mother? I usually come alone but I think she will be accompanying me from here on out"

What a way to introduce someone. "My name is Goeun, mother. Although Yohan tied the knot with me, I think it would've been better if he married his paperwork instead." Smiling a little, I imagined what it would be like to see his mother in person.

"I've heard a lot about you from your son. Just like your name, you have a heart of gold, and you are as beautiful as the spring season. I heard you like these type of flowers, I'll make sure to bring many more next time"

I watched behind him as Yohan sat down and stayed silent for a while. I didn't dare disturb him during this time, but instead, closed my eyes out of respect.

"I think we should go now, it's getting late" standing up, he picked up our stuff before grabbing my hand, catching me off guard. I walked downhill with him, trying to control this tingly feeling inside of me.

"Do you want to do anything after this? I'm free for the rest of the day" Hearing that, I thought about it seriously since I don't want to waste this precious opportunity. "Hmm, let's take turns doing the things we want today. What would you like to do first?"

As he held up our intertwined hands, confusion took over me. "Do you want me to let go? You grabbed my hand first, it's not my fault" semi-glaring at him, I was going to let go but he kept a firm hold. "That's not what I meant. You know you're impatient sometimes, not letting me finish" I thought he was annoyed at me but I saw how he tried to cover up his smile.

I wonder where he's going to take me to?

"I noticed you don't wear any rings or bracelets. Do you worry that I don't have enough money?" Laughing at his silly assumption, I examined the jewelry in front of me. "I just never liked the feeling of something weighing on my hands. But I'll gladly make an exception if you get me something"

"Let me look at all the Garakjis that you have" (garakji means a ring that's only worn by married women)

The seller, probably in her mid thirties, took out the rings before explaining it to us. "Many women buy these rings based off the season so it matches their clothing and fashion style. The jade rings represent the autumn season, so that's what I mostly have right now."

Yohan picked one out and put it on my finger before asking "Why do you think people wear their rings on this specific finger?"

"It's because people say that the fourth finger has a vein that connects directly to our heart. Isn't that romantic?" Admiring the small beauty, I showed it off to him and he nodded with a pleased expression.

"Whatever you say.." as he placed a few coins in the woman's hands, she gave us a knowing smile. "Your husband treats you so well, and mine on the other hand, lazes around at home while I do all the work. You chose well young lady"

"I do have a good eye for things-" Yohan covered my mouth before bowing at the woman. "I hope you sell lots, good day"

Part 23

"Did you think of what you want to do yet?" As we came home, an idea struck me as I looked at the target he was practicing with a few days ago. Pointing at it, I said "Teach me that". He looked over at it before rubbing the back of his neck. "Are you sure you want to learn archery? It's pretty difficult to do and I don't want your fingers hurting from the rough wood."

With a determined face, I went inside to get his bow and arrows. I also want to learn the things he loves to do. It shouldn't be too hard since Hwang Minah used to do that as well.

I made my way over to Yohan while he stared at my fire lit eyes filled with ambition. Seeing how I wouldn't give up, he softly sighed "Okay, our first lesson starts now"

About two hours passed by and I regretted my bold decision. The arrow kept drifting off the bow when I placed it in position. Then when I tried to aim and shoot, it scraped my fingers along the way. The target was totally forgotten as my only goal was to actually be able to shoot it correctly.

Yohan tried to teach me how to position it but I kept making the same mistakes and he was slowly starting to get ticked off. I could sense his bad mood as he kept silent towards the end. I'm glad he wasn't yelling at me though like how he does with his men in the training grounds. Sighing in defeat, I placed everything down before glancing over at Yohan.

"It's okay, it takes a lot of practice to become good at archery. But it also needs talent to be able to do well" I know he didn't mean much when he spoke about talent, but it somehow made me feel angry. It's as if he was telling me I have no talent in this so I should give up. In a way, I felt belittled

Turning away from him, I went back in our residence in an attempt to cool down. I know I was being childish, but I really wanted to do well today, and show him that, I too, can be as talented as his old lover.

Dinner was served and I ate quietly, earning a few glances from Yohan. "Is something the matter?" He placed his chopsticks down and I stopped eating before shaking my head no. He looked unconvinced but kept quiet as we finished the rest of our meal.

Soon it was time for bed, and Areum was busy brushing my hair. I can tell she also sensed that something was wrong today since the whole room was quiet, Yohan was looking over an important scroll and I kept my gaze down in front of the mirror.

"You can leave now" Hearing his voice, Areum put the brush down before taking her leave immediately. Playing with the ring on my finger, a few minutes passed before I heard him roll the scroll up. The brush beside me got picked up and he slowly started to brush my hair, as I sat there looking at the reflection of the mirror.

"Can you tell me why you are upset with me? Did I do or say something wrong?" I felt more relaxed once he ran his hand through my hair, softly playing with it.

"I'm more mad at myself, you don't have to worry about it, I'll be fine after a bit" Taking the brush from his hand, I placed it down on the table with a soft thud. But before I could get up from the chair, he turned me around so that I was facing him directly.

"If it's because of the earlier events, then don't be upset about it. If you want, I'll teach you until you become good at it" looking into his eyes, I could see the sincerity in them which made me feel even more embarrassed of my childish self.

"I-I can't seem to do any of the things that you take interest in. I can't ride a horse on my own without feeling sick after a while. I can't shoot arrows or handle a sword. I also can't-"

"Shh" "Instead of focusing on the things that you can't do, what about telling me about all the things that you can do" I thought about it for a moment, before shyly looking at him again.

"I can cook.."

"very delicious food"

"I can do embroidery"

"That jasmine handkerchief you gave me was beautiful"

"I can paint.."

"I'd love to see you painting something for me one day. Look, there's so many things that you are capable of doing and many more to come. So what if you aren't able to do the things I like. You can ride the horse with me and accompany me as I work on my archery and sword matches. I promised you that I would protect you, so don't force yourself to do the things you don't want"

"I think I'm going to cry" I choked up on my words hearing him appreciate and embracing me as who I am as a person.

"Oh no, I was intending to make you smile, not cry. Let's also add one thing to the list, you're also good at being a crybaby"

Smiling at that, I wiped away the tears and he unexpectedly pulled me in for a hug.

I think I'm going to add something to his list as well. He's good at comforting others...and he gives the best hugs

Part 24

The harvest festival soon arrived and I was actually really nervous. As I wrapped up the fruits and rice cakes in beautiful packaging, the idea of meeting the rest of Yohan's family and relatives felt scary. Today was the day where everyone comes together and celebrates with their friends and family.

Yohan said that we would be at mother and father in-laws house for half of the day and the rest will be our time to have fun. Giving the baskets to Areum to put in the carriage, I set off to my room to doll myself up. Wearing my light blue flowy dress, I made sure my hair was neat and presentable.

Once I came out, I saw Yohan as he was getting his horse ready. "Kkum Kkumah" walking over to them, I stroked the horse's hair before feeding him a few snacks.

"You're really going to call him that?" Staring at me with disbelief, Yohan shook his head before opening the palanquin for me. "You thought I was kidding?" I made my way inside before flashing him a smile. "You know your wife is fetching for many compliments today" As I blinked my eyes waiting for him to respond, he abruptly closed the entrance, making me scoff. He is good with words but can't say something so simple.

The trip went by smoothly, taking up only 20 minutes of our time since their residence was relatively close. As I got out and went over to the carriage, Yohan beat me to it and picked up all of the baskets.

As we walked side by side, he nudged me before saying "your smile is beautiful". Going inside, he left me in a flustered state as I didn't expect him to give me an answer. I asked him to compliment me on how I look with my outfit.."He knows how to make someone's heart flutter" muttering to myself, I also went inside with a shy smile on my face.

Giving each others gifts and our greetings, they all sat me down before introducing themselves. All of the women my age were sitting in a circle, passing around the food. I did not know that Yohan had cousins so it was fun gossiping with them for a while, up until they started to talk about my husband.

"Did Yohan tell you about that girl yet?" One of them suddenly spoke up, making the room go silent. One of the girls nudged her to stop but she shrugged it off.

"Yes, he has told me. You're talking about miss Hwang Minahssi, right?"

"I thought they were going to get married since we all know they are soulmates, but one day, she just disappeared. Minah and her mom left quietly without even telling Yohan. Can you imagine that? He was devastated, locked himself up in his room for days" Stealing a few glances at me, the girl kept going, making my blood boil even more.

"I see" Eating my rice cake, I listened as she continued her story. How does she know so much about them?? "I've heard rumors that Minah was seen with a child so we all assume that she's married and living happily."

"What do you think your husband will do if she ever shows up one day?"

I.....don't know...

That girl snickered watching my reaction and I suddenly wanted to leave this place. Everyone's eyes were on me, as if waiting for me to slip up and say something wrong.

"He's my husband right now so I don't see the issue here? I am living happily and I hope the same for Miss Minah." I got up annoyed before making my way to the kitchen area. Father in law's mother was sitting there with her friends, chattering away as they reminisced their past. Hearing their stories, I stayed with them until it was time to go.

Peeking through the little window, I saw how Yohan's eyes was searching through the crowd outside as everyone was preparing to leave. Once he caught sight of me poking my head out, he visibly relaxed and motioned for me to come over.

Saying my farewells, I stood beside Yohan, eager to leave for the festival like we had planned. Once we headed out and entered the market, it was early evening, the sun slowly setting. The stalls of food were lined up next to one another and all sorts of games were displayed. Children were playing on the streets, and entertainers were dancing, singing, telling stories, and having competitions.

"Where should we go first?" Excitingly looking around, I didn't know where to start, finding everything to be fun. "Lets not get lost first" holding my hand, he pulled me towards him and I gave him a mischievous smile. "You seem to like holding my hand often."

"That too" He started walking to a crafts shop, where it was a little less crowded, making me wonder why he was leading us there. "Are you suddenly into craft making?" Shaking his head no, he said "we have some people to meet today"

Entering the small shop, I took notice of two people who had their backs turned on us. They were wearing simple commoners clothes but the hair ornament on the lady's hair gave it away.

"They really came?" No way..

"You can turn around, she seems to recognize you immediately." He knew their covers were blown when I excitedly pointed at them. Prince Yul turned around with disappointment and Hyerin was jumping out of joy. "I won the bet, I told you she would get it right away!"

"You guys are my only close friends anyways. I just didn't know you would actually come to the festival like we had planned" Hugging Hyerin, we stayed like that for a bit, swaying side to side. The two men just exchanged glances with each other, since they probably meet every other day. Lucky bastards

"Why haven't you been writing to me lately?" she looked guilty as we parted, laughing cheekily. "I sort of might have been busy with other things" noticing her rubbing her belly unconsciously, a warm feeling blossomed inside of me.

Turning my head towards Prince Yul, I arched my eyebrow smiling and he seemed to get embarrassed judging by his pink ears.

"Congratulations, both of you" Yohan stood beside me before teasing his friend. "I can't believe a child is going to have a baby soon"

Their bickering continued as me and Hyerin made our way outside. "Are you not feeling any nauseousness when you smell or eat food?"

"No, but I do experience dizziness in the morning." She shook her head before saying "One morning, I didn't feel like getting up so Yul panicked and called for a royal doctor immediately. I thought he was exaggerating but fortunately we got to hear the good news because of it."

"Make sure to not overwork yourself and get plenty of rest. How is palace life by the way, is the people treating you well?"

Hyerin stopped before sighing in defeat. "I didn't realize there's so many people still attached to my husband. It's difficult to make them realize that I'm already by his side, and that they should back off"

Exactly.

"How about you voice your concerns to your husband? Maybe you'll come up with a solution together" Hearing myself say these words, I almost wanted to laugh at myself. I am good at giving advices but I never follow them myself.

Hyerin took it into consideration before smiling, showing me her cute dimples. "Enough of my life, let's have lots of fun today. I heard that they're doing a play soon, so let's quickly grab something to eat before heading over there"

Part 25

The play was coming to a start as everyone took their seats, clapping their hands to the beat of the music. As I followed along, I had this sudden feeling that my hand felt too empty. Once I got a closer look, I realized the ring on my finger was gone. Did I drop it?

Looking around me, there was no sight of my precious gift, leaving me dumbstruck. I have to retrace my steps.. "I'll be right back" handing Hyerin my food, I left quietly, my eyes glued to the ground.

This is like looking for a needle in a haystack It was so crowded as I kept bumping into people, apologizing along the way. Finding the crafts shop again, I entered in a rush, startling the poor owner who was wiping the furniture.

"May I take a look around sir, I think I might have dropped my ring somewhere"

Nodding, he shooed me off and I looked around, desperately hoping to see it lying around here. "I swear this is why I don't wear jewelry. How can I lose it in just a few days time? Ridiculous.." Scolding myself, I halted to a stop stumbling upon a shiny object sticking out from under the shelf.

Finally... taking it out, I wiped it before wearing it again. "I should consider getting it resized or something.."

"Ahjussi, what happened to the things I ordered from you?" In came a woman as she strided her way over confidently, her face scrunched up in annoyance.

"The ship got delayed for another day so I can't hand out anything until tomorrow." The man dusted his hands off before staring at the woman in front of him. She looked very beautiful with her chestnut colored hair flowing down her back as she put her hands on her hips.

"I guess I have no choice but to come back tomorrow. But I'm moving today so it'll be a headache..." Looking around, she finally realized they weren't alone seeing me crouched up on the floor. Quickly standing up, I gave an awkward smile "I had to find my ring..."

"Oh no worries! I was just a little confused on why you were on the floor like that" she examined me for a quick second before smiling. "I see you're married already, you look quite young. Are you here for the festival today?"

"Yes, but it's a lot more livelier this year." Realizing that I might have been gone for too long, I fastened my steps. "It was a pleasure talking with you, may I ask for your name?" As I walked up to her, I realized our height difference as she was about 2-3 inches taller than me.

"Ah it's Mayumi, what about you?"

"It's Han go-" "Kim Goeun"

A voice startled both of us as I looked at the entrance of the shop. There stood Yohan, as he sighed in relief, catching his breath.

"Maybe I'll see you next time?" The lady nodded her head before going deeper into the store with the owner, probably to look around again.

Walking over to Yohan, I showed him my ring proudly. "I finally found my ring, I didn't realize I dropped it a while ago"

"Yohan?" I grew concerned seeing him just standing there with an unreadable expression on his face. His hair looked disheveled as he took deep breaths to calm himself down. "What's wrong? Do you want me to go get water?"

He suddenly cupped my face gently leaving me flustered. His eyes held some sort of hesitation in them but my only focus was on the warmness radiating from his hands. My heart sped up thinking of what he was trying to do in our position right now. K-kiss..?

Closing my eyes in expectation, I waited for something to happen but what I didn't expect was a soft kiss being planted on my forehead. We stayed like that for a bit, not that I minded. I probably looked like a fool just standing there but I just couldn't seem to move my hands or feet at the moment.

"Don't disappear on me like that. You know how much I hate it.." He said it in such a hushed voice, no one else but me would have been able to hear it.

"I won't.....but don't we look so romantic right now?" I also whispered to him with a sly smile and he backed away almost instantly, leaving me sulking.

"Let's um head back now, Your friend was worrying about you being gone for too long" As we walked out into the busy market again, I kept regretting the fact that I ruined our moment with my remark. "Who was the woman you were conversing with back there?"

"She's apparently a customer there, we just introduced ourselves before you came in. Her name is pretty unique, Mayumi"

"That sounds like a Japanese name..." he said with his eyebrows furrowed. now that I think about it, it does.. but she had no problem speaking with me. "Anyways..I have a favor to ask you. Will you be able to get me a gate entry pass to the palace?"

"And what do you want to use it for?" Looking suspiciously at me, he waited for me to continue. "You know.., just in case if I need it" realizing that my reasoning is too weak, I quickly gave up on my request.

"Let's fasten our pace, the play will end soon and your food probably got eaten by your friend already"

"Call me Kim goeun~ again, and I'll walk faster" Teasing him lightly, I laughed out loud as he tugged me forward, ignoring my attempts at embarrassing him.

Part 26

A week passed after that fun day, the weather is now getting colder and windier. I sent Yohan to work in the morning in a sleepy state, due to the fact that we reorganized our room late into the night. The inspiration just sparked out of nowhere so I forced him to move our furniture around.

Going into his study room, I cleaned his desk out myself and put the books back on his shelf. Grabbing the scrolls, I was about to put it in his drawer when a certain envelope fell out midway. "Would it be too nosy for me to check inside?.." There was no name on the front, making my curiosity grow even more. Opening it, I pulled out the letter that was neatly folded. Scanning through the content, my eyes fixated on the bottom writing.

My mother wants to leave immediately so I have no other choice but to go. You know how much she is dependent on me. I hope you will wait for me to come back because I promise you, I will persuade her to return. I'll always wait for the day when I'll run back in your arms again, I love you Yohan

My mouth became dry as I put it back in its place, making sure it looked almost untouched. A weird silence consumed me as I put the situation together. It seems like they loved each other dearly, so why did Yohan get married to me? Now I feel like the horrible wench that stole someone else's man.

Walking away from his study, I stepped out into the garden, making my way to the swing that Yohan had personally ordered to be built. When I told him that I never sat on these things or played games when I was younger, he immediately hired someone to get to work. Chuckling, I sat down, swinging back and forth a few times.

With that kind of personality, he can make anyone fall in love with him. I just couldn't filter out my thoughts anymore, the nasty and disturbing feelings crept up to me. I'm not an angel all the time, I have feelings such as jealousy, sadness, anger, resentment, and they are all slowly starting to resurface. I kept getting thoughts like I'm not enough for him. He still loves her, that's why he kept that letter. He'll abandon you if she ever comes back. You're just a replacement.. "Goeun?"It hasn't even been a year since you knew Yohan but they've known each other for years and years. I can never beat that

"Lady Goeun?" Letting go my train of thoughts, I looked to see Areum peering down at me with concern. "Are you feeling alright my lady? You look like you have a dark cloud over your head."

"I think that cloud will start raining soon. Anyways, good luck on your chores" Patting her shoulder, I left behind a worried Areum. She never followed me though, knowing that I will not tell her anything until I feel better.

My tough side was telling me to stop acting like such a pitiful wuss and own up my title as the general's wife but my weaker side told me to just lay down in bed and whine about it until I felt better. The latter felt like a better option right now.

Instead, here I am, a while later, eating some spicy food from the small shop in the market. The stress melted away as I took a few bites, the strong flavor kicking in. Eyeing the lady who was selling homemade sweets, I made a mental note to get some later.

My next stop was to the bookstore, a place that I would probably never get tired of. I passed by the history books without batting an eye before grabbing a few romance novels. Sitting down in the corner, I began to read, intrigued by the storyline already. The rest of the afternoon, I pampered myself so I could feel like myself again.

It was early evening when I arrived home, and the first thing I see is Areum running up to me in a rush. "Cut these desserts for my husband once he comes home" handing her the bags of stuff I got, I stood there confused as she took them in a hurry. "We've had a guest over for about an hour now. She says she needs to talk to the owner of this residence and insisted on waiting."

"Then I'll have to see to it as I'm the only one present" Going inside to the dining room, I came face to face with a familiar woman sitting patiently, her hands on her lap. She was wearing a dark brown dress that went down to her calves. It looked like the outfits that female warriors wear so they can walk freely without stepping or slipping on it. Once she looked up, I recognized her immediately, her striking features can never be forgotten.

"Miss Mayumi?" She also had a look of bewilderment on her face, clearly surprised that I was the one standing in front of her. "Lady Goeun?" Sitting down, I gestured for one of the girls to get some tea for us.

"I was out for a while so I didn't know we had a guest today. May I ask why you wanted to see the owner?" The once patient woman suddenly seemed restless, her eyes wavering slightly. "Is Mister Kim your husband?"

"Yes? Did you come all the way here to ask that?" Shaking her head, she suddenly smiled throwing me off guard. "I had some work related business that I needed to discuss with General Kim. You see, I've been casted as a bodyguard for her highness. They apparently wanted a female and I fit right in the description, so I start work in a few days"

"Ah, I see" but what does that have to do with my husband? Sipping the tea that was put in front of us, we stayed silent, neither of us not knowing what to say. "If it isn't too rude of me, may I ask when you both got married? Its just that I always dreamed of starting a family too so I was curious.."

"It wasn't too long ago, but one thing led to another and boom, we got married" once my soft laughter died down, the room turned silent again, the awkwardness at its max. I didn't know the tablecloth had such pretty designs

"It's becoming dark and I better head home soon. Thank you for having me over, the tea was brewed wonderfully" As she got up, I blocked her way in confusion. "Didn't you need to speak with Yohan? He'll be home soon so you can sit with me until then."

"I'll come over maybe next time, have a goodnight Miss Goeunssi"

"You too, be careful during the way back" walking her out and sending her off, I watched as she left rather quickly, her retreating figure getting smaller and smaller. With questions still left unanswered, I closed the gate door with a heavy heart. Should I be wary of her in the future?

Part 27

Yohan arrived at home soon after and went straight to our room, me closely following behind. Taking off his coat, he didn't bother to change and laid down. "Aren't you hungry? I brought some of the desserts you liked last time."

"I think I'm more tired, but I'll make sure to eat some tomorrow"

"A guest came by saying she had some work related business with you. Remember the woman from the festival, Miss Mayumi?"

Sitting up, he was now alert, and I let out a sigh. Disappointed but not surprised. Nothing can beat his love for his work. "Why did she leave if she had something to say?"

"Beats me. She said she would start working as a bodyguard for Hyerin soon. Our crown prince really went over the top huh" Both of us started laughing, hearing how our friend is so protective over his pregnant wife. "What does Miss Mayumi look like anyways? Maybe I met her during one of my work trips but I don't really remember"

Thinking hard on how to describe her as accurately as I can, I started with her height. "She's about 3 inches taller than me, so right about here" showing with my hands, I moved on to the next topic. "She has long brown hair that comes down to her waist. Her face is more of a heart shape I think and she has more of an almond eye shape." Trying to think of what else to say, I was going to continue until Yohan interrupted me midway "Is there also a small mole under her right eye?"

"I think so.. how did you know?" Before I could say another word, Yohan was out the door with his coat in his hands. Running behind him, I tried to understand why he was in such a hurry. Finally grabbing his arm, I managed to stop him in his tracks. "W-where are you going?"

"I have to make sure" He tried to shake me off but I stubbornly held on to him. "Can you explain it to me clearly? Do we need to find her? I can help look too" I was going to grab my coat as well but he stopped me forcefully.

"Just stay here. I'll be back" I've never seen him so worked up before but I couldn't seem to grasp on to the situation. "Follow the left road, she went that way" We stared at each other in silence for a few seconds, his eyes held so many emotions but the only thing I had in mine were confusion and hurt.

Once he was out the door, I stood there as a shiver ran down my spine. "My lady?" Areum and the other workers looked worryingly at me so I gave them my best smile. "You can all go back to your rooms or go home for the day. But before that, can one of you fetch me a blanket"

For the next few hours, I sat on the staircase outside, waiting for Yohan to come home. By that time, I already figured out why he rushed out of the house without a proper plan. The only person who can get him so riled up like that is Miss Mayumi, no, Miss Hwang Minah.

It hasn't even been a few months since we got together, is it already time to go our own ways? The words of those ladies at Mother in laws house kept repeating in my head, making me overthink everything. Closing my eyes, I focused on my breathing and the sounds around me. The wind was blowing on the tree leaves, giving it a nice whooshing sound. Wrapping the blanket around me tighter, I silently wished that he would come back soon. Wasn't he sleepy? I'm darn tired and I'm this close to locking the gate so he won't come back in anymore.

I don't know how long passed but I must have dozed off because I jerked awake when I heard footsteps approaching. "How long have you been sitting here?" I barely looked up at him before saying "since you left?" Grabbing my blanket, I stood up but my legs had other plans for me. Stumbling, I closed my eyes in embarrassment. "My legs fell asleep, it'll get better in a minute. Go inside first"

"That won't do" my legs got swooped off the ground as he gently picked me up and carried me inside. Wrapping my arms around his neck, I kept quiet, there was nothing to feel happy or giddy about. His clothes smells like a woman's scent. Once we got to our room, I got down and he went in the changing room.

Going to the farthest part of the room, I laid the blanket down before grabbing my pillow from our bed. Feeling a headache coming in, I wrapped myself up before trying to fall asleep again. I ignored him as he came over to my spot before crouching down, keeping quiet. Exactly feel guilty. "I'm sorry" his voice sounded tired and gruff, but the apology felt sincere.

"Did you meet her? Miss Hwang Minahssi" opening my eyes, I saw how his eyes widened by the fact that I figured it out already. "How did you-?"

"The General wouldn't run to a random stranger in the middle of the night like his life depended on it. So I pieced two and two together, how smart of me right?" Before I could turn my body the opposite way, he held my wrist down, keeping me in place.

"Trust me, nothing happened between us tonight"

"But it could on some other night?" "Kim Goeun" I knew that I crossed the line by saying that and I know how I am acting like such a- Sitting up, I finally lost it

"I tried to understand! In fact I'm still trying to understand that you both haven't seen each other in years. I know how much you missed one another but I feel like an obstacle that's holding the both of you down. Do you not think you will regret marrying me? Will I not feel like a constant burden that you need to get rid of?" Something switched in his eyes and I felt an ominous feeling radiating from him. His hand on my wrist tightened and for once, I felt scared in his presence.

"Why do you talk as if you forced me into this marriage?! I chose on my own to make this decision and I was the one who approached you first with a proposal. So don't you dare think that I have no affection for you Kim Goeun."

"Then, do you love me?" With barely a whisper, I managed to shut him up and he was left speechless. "T-then don't touch me" as if his touch burned me, I pushed his hand away before laying back down facing the wall. His heavy breathing could be heard as he threw his coat across the room.

"F---- dammit"

Part 28

The silent treatment continued between us for five days now, where we both ignored each other's presence. I didn't send him off to work, we ate at separate times and we slept separately. I could tell everyone was worried about this sudden change of mood but I think it's better that we take time away from each other to sort out our thoughts.

Some guards came this morning saying that someone from the palace was waiting for me to come over today. It's probably Hyerin or Prince Yul.

Arriving shortly, I got escorted to the study room, where Prince Yul was writing away. "Your highness asked for my presence?" Bowing, I walked over before sitting down, obviously confused on why he asked for me.

Exchanging greetings and all those "how are you" "how's your family", he finally got to business. "Yohan told me about what's happening. I'm truly sorry, I didn't know Miss Mayumi was in fact her"

Furrowing my brows, I tried hard to understand him. "Her having a job here doesn't bother me Prince Yul. From what I've heard, she's excellent at swordery and martial arts. Isn't that the type of person you are looking for Hyerin?"

"Yes, but I also wanted your opinion before deciding to keep her. I've only met her a few times before in the past so I didn't really remember her face." Putting his brush down, he looked at me with pity, the thing I hated the most.

"I hope you can be understanding about this situation Goeun. I know it's not fair for you and I know Yohan is probably very stunned right now. He hasn't seen her for years, the lo- relationship they had was very strong. She was there for him when his mother passed, so it's hard to move on quickly."

Biting the inside of my cheek, I refrained from saying things that could hurt all of us. "So are you saying I should step away because the rightful owner came back?"

I could see the panic in his eyes as he struggled to find the right words to say. "N-No! I was just trying to tell you to not give up on him so early. Stand your ground and don't bring yourself down like that. The Lady Goeun I know is confident of herself and that is precisely why Yohan took interest in you."

I took that advice in half heartedly before nodding. "Is there anything else you called me here for?"

"Ah, yes. I was going on a small trip down south with Hyerin and we are to stay there for about a month or so. I was thinking if you wanted to go as well, it would help you relieve some stress." Actually considering it, the idea didn't seem bad, I could use a distraction.

"Then I'll gladly accept the offer. When are we leaving?"

His face brightened up, poor guy, he was probably waiting for the rejection to hit him. "It's in a few days so I suggest you start packing." Writing some more things down, he closed up the paper before handing it to me. "And could you please send this to the generals room. I really need this to be delivered to him fast" he really has the balls to ask me that, huh

Smiling, I took the scroll from his hands before giving him a stern look "And please tell this general of yours that problems that happen in the house, stays in it. Have a nice day Prince Yul"

Now walking to the Generals place, I got stopped by his guards right out front. "I'm General Kim's wife, so you don't have to inform him that I'm here"

I went inside only to be stopped by hushed voices coming from his room. Leaning closer, I tried to hear what was going on. "So you have a child?" That was definitely Yohan's voice and I can probably guess who he was talking to.

"Is that why you got married? Because you heard rumors about me?"

"Look.. you shouldn't be here. Stop neglecting your duties, or I will report today's incident"

"It's not my child... it's..my mothers. Although she's widowed, she got entangled with another man. I know...how disgraceful" silently gasping, I contemplated on whether or not I should keep listening. Once your husband has passed away, you are not allowed to remarry or get involved with another man, or atleast that's what mother told me.

"So answer me Yohan, baby, do we still have a chance?" Something snapped in me hearing her call him that so comfortably and shamelessly. Before he could respond to that, I knocked on the door before coming in, my hands gripping onto the scroll tightly.

"Goeun?" He looked surprised on how I was standing in front of them, both acting like they got caught during an affair. "I'm here to give you an urgent scroll baby."

"Oh, Miss Mayumi? What are you doing here? I thought you were Hyerin's bodyguard?" My voice laced with distaste, I made sure to let them know that I heard everything that came out of their mouths. Bowing her head, she left quickly, but I saw the frown on her face as she passed by.

Once the door was shut, my face changed so fast, even I got scared of how fake I was right now. "Prince Yul asked me to give this to you. Why don't you open it, it seems important."

I attempted to leave but he held onto my arm before opening the scroll calmly. "It says here that he's going on a trip with her highness and his dear friend lady Goeun. He also wants me to tag along with them to inspect the area with my troop. Shall I accept?"

And that's when I realized I fell right into one of Prince Yul's traps. "Amazing. You can go but I'm staying" Before I could reach for the handle of the door, I heard something being placed on the table. "Too bad, I already have the stamp to confirm our departure." With a smirk, he held up the paper proudly.

"And what if I say I'm sick on that day? No one will force me to go"

"Then I'll just have to carry you like last time" I side eyed him showing my disapproval. "I'll gain so much weight you won't be able to lift me" Snorting, he held in his laughter before looking over at me mischievously. "Don't underestimate the generals strength"

Walking out of his study, I scoffed questioning the amount of confidence this person can possibly have.

"Where's the palanquin?" Yohan glanced between me and the horse I got from the stables. "I've taken up the challenge to ride a horse like most of you."

Yohan blinked a few times before shaking his head. "The journey takes 4 days if we travel nonstop or about a week if we decide to rest a few times. Are you sure you can handle it?"

I got lessons from the young guard at our residence and he taught me the basic things I needed to know. I was told to not pack a lot because it would tire out the horses that were pulling the carriages. So it was really hard picking out clothes and necessities I'll need for a month.

"I'll manage, it's already hard for the workers walking there, it would be too tough for them carrying the palanquin." Yohan and I are talking now, but it hasn't returned to how it normally was. We answer each others questions but we don't actually engage in the conversation.

Sighing, he came over to me before handing me the rein to his horse. Taking mine, he waited for me to get on first. "Since he knows you, he will be more gentle with you"

Patting my beloved kkumah, (dream), I got on carefully, feeling Yohan's intense stare burning into me. I had to wear a warmer dress since Areum insisted that I'll freeze to death if I didn't. I let Areum and the others stay behind to take care of the house and told them to think of it as a little vacation without me.

Once he got on his as well, we headed out to our meeting point at the palace. There, at the gates, stood Crown Prince Yul on his horse, and many soldiers behind him. A large palanquin could also be seen, with Miss Mayumi next to it on her horse.

Everyone looked ready to depart, and were waiting for their general to stand by his highness's side. Looking over at me once more, he nodded his head before going to the front. Staying behind, I blended in with the others, excited to start our journey.

"Don't worry my dear horse, I'm way lighter than your master so it will be easy for you." Stroking his mane, I let him feel reassured even without Yohan by his side.

"Let's hope I don't make a complete fool out of myself"

Part 29

The days passed as we travelled endlessly, taking breaks to eat and to sleep. I finally got the taste of what my husband and all these people experience often, making me realize how ungrateful I am.

It was already time for dinner when we came to a stop, and I swear I think my behind got two times flatter than how it originally was. Sitting for so long gets uncomfortable after a while, and I also had to keep my nausea in check.

Everyone got into a line, waiting to grab their food to eat that was being cooked by the royal chef himself. As I waited for my turn, someone tapped on my shoulder lightly. "you're a noble lady and the general's wife. You can easily skip your way to the front my lady. No one will mind"

Looking back, I noticed it was one of Yohan's soldiers. They're all taller than me so I'm stuck looking at the back of people's heads most of the time. "That's unfair for all of you, we're all equally exhausted and hungry for the day. I would be angry if someone cut me in line."

Nodding his head, he then went on to the next question. "I hope this isn't too rude of me to ask but did you and our general get into a quarrel?" Furrowing my brows, I waited for him to continue.

"It's just that.. everyone's been talking about how you won't even share a tent together...Ahh I'm sorry now I feel ashamed of myself. Please act like you didn't hear me!" Covering his face, he bowed his head several times, making me flustered.

"N-no it's just that I have been dealing with insomnia lately and didn't want to disturb your general's sleep. He needs good rest in order to lead everyone safely" Making up a sweet lie, I convinced him and the people around us who were eavesdropping. Although, part of it is true

"Why are you so tiny, it took me a while to spot you" Just in time, Yohan came over to us holding his food in his hands. General privileges"You. Take this and go eat" Handing the meal over to the young man behind me, Yohan took his place, leaving me confused.

"When did you get so humble my lady? First you ride a horse although you hated the idea of it before and now you're waiting in line without complaining" Standing close behind me, he whispered so that only I could hear it. The tingly feeling didn't seem to go away as he placed his chin on my shoulder.

"You make it sound as if I'm an arrogant woman. And the last time we talked, didn't I tell you to not touch me" nudging him away, our bickering didn't stop until we joined Hyerin and prince Yul at our sitting spot.

Now that I closely looked at our meal, I realized there was meat in the soup that I didn't really like. Silently sliding Yohan's bowl to my side, I gave the meat to him and he in return, gave more of his potatoes to me. Our silent exchange was made and we started eating, ignoring the stares of the two beside us.

"You said they were not on good terms at the moment,...right?"

"I guess I had nothing to worry about."

"Goeun Unnie, I want to introduce you to my new bodyguard. Do you mind if she sits with us for a while?" Prince Yul suddenly choked on his food, grabbing the attention of the people around us. Yohan slapped his back a few times and Hyerin offered him some water.

"Th-that won't be n-necessary" coughing, his highness looked between me and Yohan out of nervousness. "Is your name Goeun Unnie?" Hyerin, obviously confused, gave him a look that probably means "what is wrong with you"

"I already met her a few times actually. She has a face you can't typically forget" She smiled at my words before signaling Miss Minah to come over. I ate in silence watching her take secret glances at Yohan. I know I can just act all lovey dovey with Yohan because I have every right to, but.. I also have a conscience.

"I'm going to head back into my tent now, have a good rest everyone." Before they could suggest otherwise, I got up and left to my sleeping spot. Putting my hair down, I sat in silence for a bit, unsure if I should sleep or not. Looking at my hair, I could see that it was starting to look less silky since I haven't washed it in days now. Oh well, we are arriving at our destination tomorrow.

Once again, I couldn't fall asleep, making me want to cry and yell at my mind to let me rest. Having enough of this, I grabbed the cloak from my small bag, putting it over my head and body before going outside.

Almost everyone had gone back to their tents, just a few were by the fire, warming up their hands and casually talking.

Going over to disturb Yohan, I peeked in only to see him reading a map of some kind. "Welcome?" He sounded surprised at my sudden arrival.

"Can I..come in?" patting the ground next to him, he motioned for me to come over. Sitting down a bit farther from him, I observed the map he was holding.

"Once we arrive tomorrow, I will take a rest for about a week before departing again. I have to leave half of the soldiers with his and her highness in their new residence. You are also ordered to stay there." Looking over at me, he explained his plans for the upcoming days. Him and his troop will have to inspect the land area near the sea. After making sure it's safe from any neighboring enemies, they will come back to enjoy the rest of their time here.

"I see..." We stayed silent for a while as I tried to gather up the courage to talk to him. The lump in my throat didn't seem to go away as I kept a tight hold of my dress. Truthfully, I've been fighting a stressful battle within myself for a while now. Although I pretend to be indifferent towards him, he's the only one I truly depended on ever since we got married. So when my source of comfort got snatched from me, I had nowhere to turn for help.

The negative thoughts and feelings have been eating me up, the anxiety I've been experiencing has taken a toll on my sleep. My left leg twitches on its own and has been jerking me awake at night. There's times when I want to cry out of nowhere, and the journey that I thought would somehow excite me, was a major disappointment.

"Yohan?" My voice already seemed to waver, and I couldn't look at him in the eye. If I do, I know I will straight up start crying.

"Hm?" ..."I think I'm having a hard time" barely speaking with a small voice, I let out the words that I had buried deep in my mind.

The map was put down and I could feel his stare on me, making me feel even more pressured.

"What's wrong Goeun?" His voice sounded softer than ever, and I could tell he was concerned right now. Because I, never really express my struggles, unless it's too much for me to bear.

"I feel disconnected from this world somehow. I can't seem to feel genuinely or completely happy. I listen to others with half interest and answer back with half sincerity. I don't want to do anything and there's this feeling of emptiness I can't describe."

"I-I'm really struggling but there's no one to help me become me again." Wiping away the tears with my sleeve, I finally managed to look up at him. "I know you're probably not comfortable with me right now, but could you give me a small hug? Even a side hug is fine"

Wrapping his arm around my waist, he pulled me closer to him. "Says the one who said no touching a while ago."

"I changed my mind" mumbling, I held onto his hand that was on my stomach, taking comfort in the warmth that he brought out. "You can't take back those words now" My body suddenly got lifted onto his lap, his arms wrapped around me securely. "You aren't allowed to"

He took me in his embrace and I hugged him back, my head resting on his chest. Hearing the sound of his heart beating as fast as mine calmed me down, and I finally felt like I could breathe freely again.

"This is why I said I didn't deserve a woman like you taking an interest in me. You are someone who should be loved and be constantly reminded of that everyday of your life."

"So love yourself first Goeun. Treat your tears as if it's worth as much as thousands and millions of gold and diamonds. Don't waste your tears on someone like me."

"But what if I want to? If I say I missed you... even though you were right beside me these past weeks, would you believe me?" Looking up at him, I saw how his eyes were a little red and glossy.

"I-" Before he could finish, a scream was heard, jolting the both of us back to our senses.

Before I could get off of him, one of his soldiers barged in, pure terror evident in his eyes. Once he saw the both of us together, his legs almost gave out on him.

"Thank the lord, my lady is here with you Sir. I thought-"

"What happened?" Both of us getting up, we hurried outside, just to see fire spreading from my tent? "Why?.." Everything turned to chaos as everyone rushed to get water to put out the fire.

"Grab a bucket or anything that can hold water. There's a lake nearby so all of you follow me"

With the order of Prince Yul, we all followed his orders quickly. It took a while to get water so once we came back, it was hard to get everything in control. Once the fire was fully out, I could tell everyone looked relieved, only except one person.

"Who dared to start a fire in my wife's place?" Yohan looked extremely shaken up as his eyes was blazing in anger. I, on the other hand, was too stunned to speak looking at the damage of my tent. Nothing inside could be preserved and the thought that I could have died If I hadn't gone to Yohan made me shudder. But no one here is an enemy? But how could it be an accident?"

Mostly everyone was quiet until one spoke up nervously. "We all wouldn't dare try to hurt my lady and thankfully, she is unharmed right now." Hyerin stood next to me with a cloth over her mouth, afraid that she might inhale the toxic things in the air. Holding her hand tightly, I managed to calm myself down.

"We will ride till we go to the residence. I don't want any of us sleeping here anymore, so even if we struggle, let's hold on a little longer" Prince Yul looked at his wife and then to Yohan for confirmation.

"Pack up and we will head out!" Heading back to get his stuff, I let go of Hyerin before giving her a reassuring smile.

Everyone was ready to go and I silently walked over to Yohan who got on his own horse. Tugging on his sleeve, I stood there quietly. As if reading my thoughts, he pulled me up easily.

"Who do you think did it?" He stiffened up at my question before letting out a shaky breath. The only suspicion I have is of Minah because god knows what a person can do out of jealousy or hatred. But if I ever mention that, no one would believe me, even I have a hard time believing that.

"I don't know...but if you were in that fire, I wouldn't have hesitated to jump in to save you. Because the thought of this world without my Goeun is sickening."

Part 30

I have never felt so happier seeing a hot bath and comfortable bed ready for me to use. Everyone was exhausted and ready to sleep, since we arrived many hours after midnight. Once I laid my head on the pillow, I went to sleep almost instantly, so I guess my insomnia is solved?

Waking up from my long slumber, I realized it was already afternoon, and my body finally felt well rested. Stretching, I turned around just to almost get a heart attack by the sight in front of me.

Yohan was by the door grabbing the platter of food from someone, ..shirtless. Closing my eyes immediately, I ran inside the wash room hurriedly. Washing my face by the basin, I sat down on the ground for a minute, embarrassed of myself. I'm a grown woman but I freaked out just by looking at his upper body.

Of course it would be natural to be surprised. I'm not a pervert who had stared at others bodies before. Going back out in a calmer manner, I subtly tried to not look directly at him.

"Why aren't you coming here to eat?" I could hear his voice as he watched me tidy up the bed. Grabbing a thin blanket, I trudged over to him before wrapping it around his body. Arching his eyebrow, he looked at the blanket before chuckling.

"You-looked cold, so I did you a favor. Who doesn't wear clothes when it's chilly outside" Mumbling, I sat down next to him before eyeing the food. "What's this?"

There was two bowls that had dark liquid inside of it. "You're not poisoning me right?"

Yohan rolled his eyes before taking one and gulping it down in one go. He didn't seem to have a reaction to it so I naturally thought it would taste pretty good. I also drank some until the bitter flavor kicked in, almost making me gag in disgust. You betrayer

"Drink it all, it's good for your health. Then I'll give you this." Holding the sweets in his hand, he waited until I drank the last drop before handing it to me. Taking it gratefully, I popped one in my mouth, wanting the bitter taste to be gone. "Do you drink these often?"

"Sometimes, it helps my body heal when I'm not in my best condition."

"Do you get hurt often?"

"Not that much, just a few times" Looking over at his palm, the white faint line stood there as a reminder that he is constantly put in life threatening situations. I do not want to see the day he goes off to a battle or war, because I will not be able to handle it.

"Which injury was the most painful?" He thought about it before taking off the blanket, giving me full access to his handsome looking body. We are in a serious mood here Goeun, snap out of it

"This one here" guiding my hand to his abdomen, he let me touch the wider scar that he had. It looked awfully like a scar made by a knife or a sword, making me wince. Softly patting that part, I looked at him with my face scrunched up in concern. "That must've hurt badly. You better have asked his majesty to give you many months off. I would've demanded it"

"I want to show you one more" nodding my head, I waited for him to guide my hand to that area. I furrowed my eyebrows when he placed it on his cheeks, making me confused. "But I don't see a scar here?" Caressing his cheeks, all I could feel was the smoothness, and so I looked even closer at that area. Maybe a paper cut???

"There's nothing there"

"Then why-?" "I just wanted to see your reaction" Should I slap him?

"Now it's your turn"

Blinking my eyes, my face flushed realizing what he meant. "I am not going to take off my clothes" His laughter erupted throughout the whole room, making me feel even more embarrassed. "I'm just joking my lady"

If I had any physical scars, then I wouldn't have passed the first round of the selection in the beginning. Huffing in annoyance, I resumed eating, hearing him still letting out bursts of small laughter at my reaction.

"Ahh, I missed this"

"Hm?" Looking over at him, I tried to understand what he meant by that. His gaze felt different from before as he smiled tenderly at me. "I missed being with you like this"

Is this a confession? My eyes dilated in both shyness yet in excitement. Trying to figure out his next move, my heart jumped seeing him leaning in slowly, his eyes slowly looking down to my lips. Lifting my chin ever so slightly, he slid his finger over my lower lip, his touch leaving such a great impact on me.

"You're my happy place, so don't ignore me anymore." Placing gentle feathery kisses on my forehead, then to my cheeks, and even to the tip of my nose, his eyes darkened some more. However, his next move never came as we stared at each other with both desire and affection. Something was blocking him from continuing and I could see the conflict and desperation in his eyes.

"What's keeping you from coming to me?" Why do we struggle so much to do the things others consider easy... Stroking his cheeks, I gave him one final look before muttering "Then just for today, I'll be the bad person"

Placing my lips on his, I tilted my head for better access, the gentle yet soft pressure making me want more of this addicting feeling. Our lips came together just right as he took control, grabbing the back of my head.

The kiss turned more aggressive as I slowly ran out of breath, my brain feeling fuzzy as I felt his lip quiver against mine. An unexpected muffled noise came out of my throat when his hands started wandering over my body, a weird sensation building up inside of me.

Pulling away, I suddenly felt shy under his gaze even though I was the one who made the first move. Taking my hands off of his bare chest, as if now realizing, I smiled at him innocently.

"You are one dangerous woman" kissing the tip of my nose, he swooped me up in his arms in an instant. ....

Part 31

..."Come back safely" Sending him off after our week long beautiful rest, it was time for him to go.

"Tch, you make it sound as if I'm going off to war. I'll be back soon" He was taking a handful of soldiers to inspect the area near the sea because it's very close to where we are located. Letting out a sigh, I slipped a small pouch in his pocket. "What is that?" He went to open it but I stopped him before saying "it's a norigae"

His face turned into a scowl before trying to hand it back to me. "You know these are only worn by women" We fought over it for a minute, him handing it to me and I, putting it back in his pocket.

"I Know I know, that's why I put it in a pouch because I knew you wouldn't like the idea of it. It's a good luck charm and I figured you need it more than me"

"Just wear it for my sake hm? I'll feel a lot more reassured." Finally giving up at the end, he let me do whatever I wanted. "You just need to trust this general's skills"

Once they left, I was stuck as the third wheeler with Hyerin and Prince Yul. Whenever I tried to hang out with her, his highness was always trailing behind us like a lost pet. Then there was Miss Minah who I couldn't help but feel uncomfortable around. Ever since Yohan left, she has been openly showing her dislike towards me.

When Hyerin left to go on her little date with her husband, she put Miss Minah in charge of protecting me, no matter how many times I refused. So here I am, stuck with her in silence, as I continued drawing a portrait. A while passed before I heard her let out an annoyed sigh.

"I know we both don't like each other but atleast put some effort into hiding it" Putting the ink down at last, I crossed my arms waiting for her to speak up.

"You know who I am so you must also know why I'm in distress" Gripping onto her sword, she looked down at me with hatred.

"Miss Minahssi, I don't understand why you are mad at me when I'm his rightful wife. I did not have an affair with him or become his mistress when he was with you. I respect the fact that you were his lover before but that doesn't mean you are still supposed to own that title"

Before she could interrupt, I kept going, finally letting out the things I wanted to say to her.

"You left him with a note that said to wait for you but you didn't even wait for his reply back then. You just blindly assumed that he would be ready to accept you whenever you returned, but unfortunately, everyone moves on one day. Patience runs out and the heart grows tired, and sometimes, the once strong flames of love die down over time."

The once strong gaze in her eyes seemed to have faltered as I saw a broken girl in front of me for the first time. "I never chose to leave him and you know that." Directing her anger onto me, I let her do so, as I continued to draw on the paper delicately.

"Atleast I would've felt less bitter if he had chosen someone.....better." Well that hurt my pride. "I've known him for most of my life and know everything about him-"

"Then I'll just have to spend the rest of my life getting to know him then, and vice versa." She was quiet for a moment before I heard her footsteps, indicating that she was leaving. "I consider myself to be very competitive and will do whatever it takes to bring victory onto my side. I hope you keep that in mind, Han Goeun" Her words came off as a warning to me, and I'm sure she wanted me to interpret it in that way.

I was slowly starting to get ticked off by her attitude towards me, when I've been trying my best to approach this situation with maturity. Sighing, I looked at the ring in my hand, worry taking over me for some reason. Come back soon...Yohan

---3rd person pov:

"Your highness! Your royal highness!!" Prince Yul's eunuch came rushing in unannounced into Prince Yul's room, which was very unlike him. With a shaky voice, he said "General Kim and his soldiers got attacked by the Japanese troops at dawn, one of them came running back with severe injuries."

Worry filled Prince Yul's heart as he heard the horrible news of them being in danger. "So what's the situation so far, how much backup do they need?"

"I-I cannot say. The man said that there's no one to lead them at the moment" Prince Yul sprung up in horror hearing those words come out of the Eunuch's mouth. His closest friend, the most capable man by his side, couldn't have possibly...

"Notify all of our men, we are heading out this instant" Bowing down to the ground, the poor man tried to stop him, yelling out a cry of plea. "You mustn't your highness! Your safety comes first and you should not ever get injured. Please reconsider!"

"Move this instant or your head will be the first one gone. Do you dare to disobey me?!"

Cowering in fear, he let go of him hesitantly. Everything seemed to pass as a blur as a handful of guards were placed at the residence before the rest left with his highness. Hyerin was quite shaken up at the sudden tragedy but hurried off to find Goeun, knowing that she would not take the news well. Her personal bodyguard on the other hand, was on the verge to leave all her duties and rush off to go help and fight.

"We should've known that the Japanese were waiting for the right time to attack. We are so close to the border near the sea…" Her mind was everywhere as she ran behind Hyerin, as she worried for Yohan's safety.

1st person pov:

"Where's your General ?" My heart sped up looking at the young soldier who had came back alone, as they bandaged up his arm.

Once he didn't reply back, I started hyperventilating, panic rising in me at an alarming rate. "Where's my husband? Why are you so quiet?!"

"I-I don't know either. One minute we were all sleeping soundly and the next minute, they raided our camp with three times the amount of soldiers. Our general was nowhere to be seen, we were left to fend on our own" His body shaking, he held his head with his hand, and the royal medic looked at me with disapproval. "He needs rest right now, I suggest you leave for the time being."

I got kicked out mercilessly, leaving me in shock and in denial. "W-what am I supposed to do now? Where am I supposed to go?" Tears welled up in my eyes as I looked around me as if expecting to find an answer somewhere, anywhere.

"Goeun!" I felt someone pull me in their embrace but I couldn't care less as everything was muffled out, the only thought of the attack circling around my head.

I came back to my senses as someone shook my body, pulling me back into reality, a pair of brown eyes were staring into mine in rage and disgust. "What is crying going to do in this situation. Will it bring him back? Will it?!" Minah squeezed my shoulders tightly as I was now alert, ready to listen to her.

"I'm going out there to fight and find him, you can stay here crying or playing around with that brush of yours. This is exactly why you are useless, place my words deep inside that head of yours." Shoving me aside, she walked off in the other direction, taking out her sword with a new lit determination in her eyes.

"What in the world is wrong with her?!" Hyerin stood by my side after regaining from the shock. What she said was harsh, but it's all completely true. "Hyerin, can you watch this residence on your own for a while?" Looking over at my closest friend and sister, I squeezed her hands tightly.

"No. It's too dangerous out there, you are not going to follow her"

Looking over at the royal medic, I knew what I had to do. "But staying here will be torture for me Hyerin. I'll be back soon" Patting her little baby bump, I walked into the room in front of us with a new plan formed in my head.

"I will need you to tell me the location of the camp you had. And I will need you to come with me to the market." They stood confused trying to understand what I was trying to do or atleast wondering what I can do as I'm just a lady.

"We need to get as much supplies, bandages, and medicines as possible to help the injured. So please, I need your full cooperation on this"

Part 32

We hurried off to the market and grabbed a carriage full of things they may need. Attaching it to the two horses, we headed out in full speed, with the map in hand.

Once we arrived at the scene, my eyes widened at the amount of people injured and in pain. "Please disregard the fact that I'm a lady and take me in as your assistant for today" Bowing my head, I let the royal physician take me under his wing as we set off to work.

Carrying all the things inside the camp, I got everything ready. Placing the blankets on the ground and taking out the bandages, people started to come in or got carried in unconscious.

"Hold him down while I pour this on his leg. It will sting a whole lot" I winced as the man let out a painful cry and gripped onto my shoulder in pain. "It's okay, you'll be alright soon" I kept chanting that to all of the soldiers as we helped them one by one. Observing the royal medic, I gained some basic knowledge on how to disinfect and bandage up a cut. He did the more serious injuries that required more skill.

We ran around about half of the day tending to everyone. As I bandaged up someone's arm, I questioned him hesitantly. "Where did His highness and the rest go?" His eyes were closed as he sat down weakly. "They chased out the rest of the enemies and are now in search of the General."

I paused for a moment letting out a breath I didn't realize I was holding. To be honest, I was so scared of the fact that I might find Yohan laying down lifeless on the ground. Knowing that he might be alive somewhere, kept me a bit sane.

"What do you think happened to him?" My voice cracking a little, I finished up giving him his treatment. "I don't know.. but I fully trust that he didn't abandon us. No matter what anyone says, I have full faith in our general."

His words seemed to have comforted me a bit as I smiled at that. "Me too"

The suspicious thing that I noticed was that no one had died, which is a good thing of course. However, I noticed that they were attacked but at certain spots that wouldn't put their life on the line. Handing out water for everyone, I also handed out more blankets since nighttime was approaching.

I prepped up something fast for everyone to eat, even if it was a small amount. By the end of it, the royal medic and I was exhausted, but seeing everyone alive and slowly healing, made me realize that it was all worth it.

"Are you holding up alright Lady Goeun?" He sat next to me as we sat by the fire, putting the medical tools in the boiling water.

"Thank you for all that you did today, you were really cool" I managed to avoid the question and lighten up the mood as he gave me a small smile.

"That is my job, you know. You also did really well today. Rest up now, I'll finish the rest" patting my shoulder proudly, he let me go to rest for a while.

Putting a blanket down in the corner, I sat down and scanned everywhere emptily. My face felt expressionless as I failed to fall asleep. Atleast crying would've felt better but that didn't seem to come out as well as I stared blankly at my hands.

I did the most I could do, so please come back to me. Come back safely and tell me how much of a good job I did.....After a few hours, Prince Yul came back with Minah right behind him. I can't imagine how mad he would be for us leaving Hyerin's side but I don't think he was considering that at the moment.

Seeing our current condition, he gave me a slight nod before coming down his horse. "What happened?" Scrambling up, I rushed over to him, scanning everyone's faces.

"They escaped by boat to the other side. We're in no condition to go in there. And, I couldn't manage to find him, I'm sorry" my hands fell to my sides as I felt the need to not bother him anymore.

The night passed as Prince Yul and his most trusted soldiers stayed up to think of a strategy or a single plan that can benefit us. Minah also squeezed herself in that group saying that she has lived in Japan before so she will certainly be of help.

Instead of laying down wide awake, I checked up on the soldiers to make sure they had no fevers. If they did, it could mean a sign of an infection from their wounds.

When I was getting a new cloth for someone, an arrow was shot near our camp, making all of us jolt in surprise. Some of the guards rushed to find the source of it. I guess their side sacrificed one of their people because they instantly got caught by our soldiers. Prince Yul came out before grabbing the piece of paper that was tied to the arrow. I saw how his face etched into a frown before he looked at me wearily.

Going over to his side, I read the note before grabbing the hem of my dress in shock. I suddenly felt nauseous as I failed to describe the feeling bubbling up inside of me.

You have eight days to get your majesty to sign the treaty between your nation and ours. Then, we will release the man, unless, you don't care whether he lives or dies.

"They're talking about Yohan, a-aren't they? What treaty are they talking about? Do you know about this?" I looked to Prince Yul for answers to only see him rub his temples in frustration.

"It will take about 4 days if I ride nonstop to the palace and 4 to come back. But my father... he wouldn't sign it so easily if it meant sacrificing one person for it. This is more of a loss for us since we will have to agree to all their terms in this treaty."

We stood in silence as I finally felt tears forming in my eyes. I felt so stressed out and knew that we had just hit our heads at a dead end. The king could easily cover this up saying that the general sacrificed his life honorably for the nation. Yohan, you...really cared for the people, is this how they will pay you back?

"Then we won't follow what they say. Let's form a plan to get Yohan back ourselves. And then if we have to, we will go into battle." Minah stood in front of us with a serious expression. "How would we do that?" His highness perked up at another option that we could use right now.

"First. We find out where they confined him"

Part 33

A bout 6 of us stood in a circle as I opened up the map I had brought with the royal physician.

"Our best guess is that they probably confined him in the boat for now and will keep him close to the borders of their land. They know that they caught someone in a higher rank and would think that we will instantly agree to their terms." She pointed at the sea between our land and theirs, and the sea separating us.

"So how would we cross over without being caught?" One of the men questioned Minah as if she was asking for a death wish.

"There's a boat a bit farther from here that takes you to their land illegally. Don't ask me how I know." She eyed all of us as we suspiciously looked at her. "If I can get across, then I'll be able to track them down and save him." She sounded very sure of herself as she explained the plan carefully.

Prince Yul furrowed his eyebrows before shaking his head. "This plan has too many holes and risks. We can't just trust you to solely save him when you can get killed too."

"Exactly, I'm willing to die for him if this plan goes under." She looked over at me as she said this, as if challenging me.

"How many people do you want to take? Or let me rephrase that. How many people are willing to go?" Most of them stood silently and Prince Yul gave me a stern look as if telling me to not speak up.

"Then what's our backup plan if this doesn't work?"

"Or... what Miss Mayumi said can be the backup plan. Our real plan can be to negotiate with them first. Mayumi can be the interpreter and that way, we can ask for more time and add in our terms as well" His highness's plan sounded more solid so we all agreed with that first.

The man that had gotten caught became our link to communicating with the other side.

―――

"What can I do to help?" The morning after, I stopped Prince Yul right before they were about to depart again.

"Take care of the people here and yourself. You're doing more than enough. And please, check up on Hyerin today. I'm worried that she is all on her own"

"Okay, you all stay safe and bring back good news for us soon. What will I say to Hyerin if you get hurt?" Nodding his head, they set out, promising that they would be back by tonight.

Today, we cleaned up some of the mess before rebuilding some of the tents for sleeping. The royal medic left to the market for more things and I checked up on Hyerin in the meantime.

I wish I could take more soldiers to the residence but since they are injured, some can't walk back here and need absolute rest. I'm holding up strong for everyone at the moment and I don't want them to feel even worse than they already are. The last thing I want is for them to think of me as a burden.

Eating a few pieces of bread, I sat alone at the camp, waiting for them to come back soon. I wonder if they fed him something.. He already has too many scars, please don't hurt him anymore.

When they came back, they informed me that they succeeded in negotiation thanks to Miss Minah. They came up with the terms and wrote the scroll down. Now all it needs is his majesty's approval...

I expected them to sound happier when delivering this news but something felt off, leaving me in confusion. Later that night, I overheard them talking among themselves, worry evident in their tones.

"They didn't even want to talk with us, why would you lie like that? They obviously took the General to fish out all the strategies he has in plan for the upcoming battles and then kill him. The treaty is just a fake cover up. They knew we would never sign it"

Covering my mouth from gasping, the tears wouldn't stop flowing down as my heart ached as if it was getting ripped out.

"Do you think it was easy for me to lie?! I could never be able to tell Lady Goeun that her husband is likely being tortured or even dead at this very moment. My best friend is over there in the enemy's hands probably willing to die for his nation without spilling a thing. And here I am, useless. Unable to persuade my father or the enemies" Prince Yul's voice faltered and I could tell he broke down as well, leaving me feeling numb.

"That's it. We are going with my plan now, whether you like it or not. I'm going to bring him back here and then you can handle the rest of the problems, whether it's going to battle or persuading his majesty." Minah's voice sounded fierce as always, which I was thankful for at the moment. We need someone like her to hold up the team when it's falling apart.

When Minah stepped out, she realized that someone was eavesdropping on their conversation. "Perfect, I'm glad you heard it. I don't need to repeat myself twice." Grabbing my wrist, she dragged me inside the woods before letting go.

"If I bring him back and we are both alive, then let me be with him now. I deserve that much don't I?"

I stared into her eyes before another single tear streamed down my face. An unexpected laugh came out of me as I stared at her in both disbelief and sadness. "Are you trying to make a deal with me? Haven't I suffered enough?"

"You think I haven't suffered all those years without him? I'm dying inside thinking that he might already be dead in that boat."

Her eyes turned glossy and I laughed more in irony. Who would've thought that we would have such a twisted fate with one another. "You know.. unnie, I really hate you" wiping away the tears, I turned away only for her to pull me back with her hand on her knife.

"The feelings are mutual. So once I succeed, do all of us a favor and leave"

How did Yohan like such a person like you...or is she just like this towards me? For some reason, the fire accident from before slipped in my brain at this very moment.

"Were you the one who started that fire?" Her glint seemed to have changed as she smiled rather scarily at me. "I knew you weren't in there when I did what I did. I had my reasons.."

I slapped her hard in the face from the pent up anger, resentment, sadness, and fear that I've been bottling up. "I've had enough of this, stop treating me like a rag doll because I too, can be as scary and disgusting like you."

Part 34

Minah left with a few of the best trained soldiers to carry out our last resort, the final mission. We all moved back into the residence we were staying at with the soldiers, and I instantly locked myself up in my room.

Suddenly, the sight of my painting and drawing tools, the embroidery needle, the hair accessories, and all my pretty dresses looked sickening to me. "What's the point of all this" throwing it all on the ground one by one, I looked at the small mirror that I had thrown harshly just a minute ago. My reflection looked cracked and the person shown looked broken as well.

"If I knew that these things would never help you, I would've never bothered to learn any of this.".…."Goeun, please come out, I'm so worried about you" Hyerin was behind the door, repeatedly telling me to come out and atleast eat.

It suddenly turned silent as the door was forcefully pushed open before his and her highness came in to the mess in my room. I sat there emotionless, unable to atleast smile to ease their worries. Hyerin pulled me in for a tight hug, her soft sobs could be heard. She stroked my hair before rocking us back and forth for a while.

"If you want Yohan to come back, then pull yourself together Goeun. Do you think he would want to see you like this?" Prince Yul's words spoke for the all of us, as a reminder that we should all keep it together, but I wasn't doing a very good job at that.

"Atleast eat two spoonfuls, you can do that for me right?" Hyerin whispered in my ear and I finally looked at the both of them before nodding.

3rd person pov:

Yohan looked up at the small confined room as he had his hand and legs tied up for some time now. "Is it daytime or nighttime?" The bleeding in his head had dried up and the bruises left on his body were aching to touch.

When they were at the camp, everything was normal and going smoothly. They were preparing to depart the next day to go back to enjoying their vacation, but look at where he had ended up. Softly chuckling, he looked at the guards who were standing outside the door, not even sparing a glance in his direction.

I'm going to die from dehydration at this rate he thought before trying to break free from the ropes. They had questioned him about the military tactics for days now and realizing that he won't mutter a word, they decided to abandon him here for now. He fought back a lot and tried to escape but there were too many people and he was outnumbered.

I wonder what they're all doing right now... are they looking for me?" His mind drifted off to the one person that kept him sane while he was locked up in here. From her beautiful features.. to her cute little smile... to her long silky hair, he wondered if she was God's favorite.

Picturing her crying face where her lips naturally turn into a pout broke his heart into pieces, as he closed his eyes to get rid of that image. "I should've treasured my beautiful woman more...my Goeun....my delicate yet strong wife"

A while passed as Yohan dozed off from a horrible headache forming, his throat parched and vision a little blurry. It only felt like he slept for a few minutes when his shoulder was being harshly shaken.

"Kim Yohan, you're not dead are you?" Finally waking up, his eyes adjusted to see Hwang Minah in front of him, with her hair a mess and her face veil slightly crooked. She let out a sigh of relief before cutting the ropes fast, looking over her shoulder a few times.

"Hurry up!" A whisper could be heard from outside as Minah put his arm over her shoulders to stand him up. "Can you walk?"

He nodded and they set out as fast as they could. That's when Yohan finally processed the situation, when he saw most of the soldiers knocked out unconscious and a few of his soldiers looking at their general with teary eyes.

When they were one step closer to escaping, a hurdle of guards circled them hurriedly, making Minah roll her eyes in frustration. "Let's get this done fast and leave. ☐☐☐☐☐☐☐☐."

Whatever she told them seemed to have ticked them off because the next thing they do is take out their swords and charge at them.

"Well thank you for pissing them off" grabbing the extra knife in Minahs pockets, Yohan got into a good stance before trying his best to defend and attack. "My pleasure" Minah smirked before slashing her sword at them, skillfully blocking their attacks.

They all got out of the building before hurriedly following Minah's lead. Yohan stood stunned as he saw a boat ready for them to leave in. "Don't be too amazed by me" winking in his direction, she helped him onto the boat before they sailed off, ready to go back to their homeland.

"Do you know how much planning had to be done to get you out as sneakily as-"

Her words seemed to have been blocked out as Yohan finally fell unconscious, his body giving out on him. They all panicked as his head hit the hard floor with a thump, making them wince in pain.

Arriving at their own land, Minah paid the owner of the boat a few bags of coins, which he took with a smile on his face. "I hope I never see your face ever again" Minah smiled back at the owner before remembering the huge slash on her arm that was bleeding heavily.

Putting pressure in that area, she gave Yohan to the other men before making their way back to the residence, ready to show them that they came back victorious.

Today was the eighth day, the last day of the "supposed" negotiation. Prince Yul told me that he sent out a letter informing his majesty about this and was waiting for them to bring backup.

The house was gloomy as everyone waited outside anxiously, hoping to see atleast a strand of their hair. Something

The amount of relief I felt when I saw a few figures approaching was an understatement as everyone rushed to their side for help. Minah collapsed in exhaustion with a horrible gash in her arm that was bleeding through her shirt.

My eyes landed on Yohan and my legs immediately started moving on its own. One of the men were carrying him on their backs as he was unconscious and I immediately showed them the room to lay him down in.

His highness called for the physician to check his pulse and condition after they treated the emergency of Minah's injury. Sitting beside him, I grabbed a hold of his hand, still not realizing that he's here in front of me, alive.

The doctor told everyone to leave and I insisted on staying, wanting to see the injuries that he had to go through all alone. The bruises on his face was slowly going down but the ones on his body were more severe. The blood on his head and hair showed me how much he had struggled out there.

The doctor got to work, and I grabbed a basin of warm water and a bunch of cloths. Wiping away all the dirt and sweat, I looked over at the physician. "Please give him the best medicine and the best salve that will heal these bruises and cuts fast."

"I'll try my best. Let's just hope there is no internal bleeding. Or else it will get more complicated"

After he left the room, I gave him water and medicine before putting some porridge next to the bed, unsure of when he would wake up. I don't know the amount of times I prayed for them to come back safely, but it all felt worth it seeing them again.

Laying down next to him, I pushed the strands of his hair out of his face before grabbing hold of his pinky finger. "I feel like if I touch you any more than this, you're going to be in pain. I want to hug you so badly, so please get better faster."

Part 35

It's been three days and he still hasn't woken up, which scared me immensely. However, the royal physician said that his health was improving just fine, so that put me at ease.

Applying the salve on him again, I looked over at the other new bottle that I had bought today. With a sigh, I grabbed it before making my way out and into the room across the hall. Knocking on the door, I made my way inside to see Minah resting, with a bandage around most of her left arm.

"How are you feeling?" Before I could come closer to her, she stopped me with her hand. "With what business are you here for?" Putting the salve next to her, I sat down a bit farther from her. "This will make the scarring lighter each time you use it, make sure to put it on two times a day."

There was an awkward silence as we both avoided eye contact, before I finally spoke up. "You know, Miss Hwang Minahssi, I was always jealous of you"

"The way Yohan described you before was like an angel and a tough warrior mixed into one. The talent you possess is also very admiring to others and your bravery is no joke. I really envy all those years you spent with him because it hasn't even been a year for me."

"Why are you saying all this?" She looked at me in confusion which I smiled in return. "Yohan will be lucky to have you again."…….Packing up a few of my things from the drawer, I looked over at my husband for the last time, afraid that if I look for a second too long, I would not have the courage to step out of this room. Grabbing a shirt of his, I also packed that in there, wanting to remember his scent when I miss him. It's okay, you'll be over me soon, like tripping over a pebble and regaining your balance quickly.

Once everyone had gone to sleep, I left quietly, knowing that my life will never be the same again. I will never meet someone like Yohan and I would never meet friends like Hyerin or Prince Yul. Maybe if I'm lucky, I'll be able to take Areum with me, wherever I'm going.

As I took every step away from the residence, my mind was screaming for someone, anyone, to notice me and stop me in my tracks. Maybe, just maybe, if they asked me what I was doing late at night and escorted me back inside, I would've followed their instructions in a heartbeat.

But no one did..

Yohan's Pov:

I was suddenly placed into battle with neither a weapon or shield, leaving me defenseless. Clashing of swords could be heard as I struggled to find something to protect myself with.

The air felt humid and the stench of blood could be smelled everywhere. Before I could realize what was happening, I saw Goeun right in the middle of the battle, looking over at me with a smile on her face. Right behind her, a man was charging at her in full speed, aiming at her back with his sword.

"WATCH OUT" I so badly wanted to warn her and scream those words, but nothing would come out of my mouth. My steps were so slow and felt heavy, as if my legs were being swallowed by the ground beneath me. Before I could reach her in time, the sword pierced through her back, her face scrunched up in pain as she let out a painful scream.

Time seemed to turn back to normal as I ran in full speed before slashing the man mercilessly. Now holding Goeun in my arms, I put pressure on the area as she bled out horribly, her face pale and sweaty.

"No.. no.. no you'll be alright baby just stay still. I'll call someone for help" My hands trembled in fear as I looked around for any familiar faces.

"Y-yohan, it hurts" She gripped onto me lightly, her energy slowly deteriorating. "Keep your eyes open Goeun, don't you dare close them." Before I could carry her up, she stopped me weakly.

"It looks like I'll have matching scars with you" Smiling at me for the last time, her eyes fluttered closed, leaving me in a state of shock. "Goeun?"

"Kim Goeun. Answer me right now" Cupping her face, I didn't know what to do as I embraced her tightly, hot tears flowing down my cheeks as I shook my head in denial.

"Wake up, what am I going to do without you? Wake up hm?" Her body was still and the blood kept gushing out, staining my hands and clothes in crimson red.

"Don't leave me like this, I promise I'll do better. I'll be better, I didn't even get to tell you how much I love you" Holding her fragile hands, I kissed them softly, gaining comfort from the fact that it was still warm.

Looking in front of me, a soldier was making his way over with a killing intent, and a smile went on my face unknowingly. "You came at the perfect time"

Closing my eyes, I waited for the impact to come, already ready to leave this wretched world. --Opening my eyes, I was now in a different place, as tears kept flowing down my cheeks endlessly. Looking over next me, I saw Goeun sitting next to me with a worried expression. Quickly getting up, I pulled her into my embrace before stroking her hair. It was just a dream, it was just a dream. You're safe in my arms.

However.. the hug felt different, way too different for my liking. Goeun is like a perfect fit for me when I take her in my embrace and her scent is a lot more different than this. Then who am I hugging?... My eyes snapped open before I pushed them away only to come face to face with Minah instead of Goeun.

"What are you doing here?" I finally came back to my senses after looking around my surroundings.

"How are you feeling? You've been in bed for 4 days now. Do you recognize me?" Handing me some water, she checked on me before getting up to probably call the doctor. Before she could leave, I grabbed her wrist in a hurry.

"Where's my wife?"

Part 36

"I'll call for the doctor and his highness. They've also been worried sick. You've been in and out of consciousness for a while now." Ignoring my question completely, she tried to step away only for me to grab onto her even more tightly.

"Bring my wife over here as well" she glared at me before running a hand through her hair.

"Can you please stop talking about your wife for a moment. I'm trying to care for you here" The rudeness she was showing threw me off guard as I stared at her in disbelief. "If you won't tell me, I'll go find her myself" Getting up, I attempted to leave until she blocked my way in panic.

"She had some errands to run, she'll be back soon"

Although confused, I decided to trust her words for now before sitting back down. Out of all people..She wouldn't lie to me

She insisted that I laid down before bringing me some water and porridge. Glancing at her arm and our surroundings, I tried to piece two and two together.

"Was it your plan to save me by boat? Was there any casualties?"

Running a hand through her hair, she let out a soft sigh. "We- lost a soldier along the way but other than that, everyone else is safe and healing."

"I see.." A weird awkwardness filled the air, something that I've never experienced with Minah before. I couldn't think of anything to say and she too was being a lot more fidgety.

"Do you want me to apply something on your bruises? I'll be sure to do it carefully" Getting up, she grabbed the salve and was about to open it but I stopped her mid-way.

"I can do it myself, you're also in no condition to be caring about me. You can step out now, and inform Goeun when she comes back."

Chewing her bottom lip, she looked conflicted before getting up slowly. "Then, have a good rest. I will check up on you later"

Scanning our room, a weird feeling seeped through me seeing this place a bit more empty than usual. Her things were not placed in the spot it usually was, making me feel concerned.

With a horrible headache, I laid back down before closing my eyes, hoping for her to come home to me soon. I bet she will come running to me to check my condition. With a small smile and some wishful thinking, I fell into a light slumber once again.

My eyes flickered open only for me to notice that the sun was setting, the sky getting darker. Getting up with a bit of struggling, I was about to open the door when Minah came in with a surprised look on her face.

"What are you doing up? You are still strictly on bed rest"

"Where's Goeun at?"

Taking a deep breath, she avoided eye contact with me, something she always did when she felt guilty. "I'll be honest with you....she left without telling anyone. None of us know why"

"Stop lying to me and tell me where she is or I will go out there to find her myself"

She blocked my way forcefully, not letting me go out, and spoke in an irritated voice.

"She's gone"

I stopped in my tracks as my heart sped up in fear. A dreaded feeling coursed through me as the dream from today was still vividly etched into my mind. "Be more elaborate,What happened to her? Is she hurt?"

Crossing her arms, she let out a scoff before pointing at her arm. "Aren't you maybe supposed to have a conversation with me regarding our escape. Why don't you ask how we got out of there alive? Or what efforts I went through to get you out of there?"

Closing my eyes, I calmed myself down, trying to understand it one step at a time. "I know you and a few other guards got me out somehow and we went back on boat. I know you got hurt, so I clearly told you that you are in no condition to be caring about me. "

I don't know what she was expecting to hear but she looked displeased with the situation.

"Kim Yohan. Why...why aren't you more concerned about me? I thought we loved each other?" She attempted to place her hand on my cheek which I instantly swatted away.

"That's the thing. I used to have feelings for you. I thought we already talked about this in my study a while back?" Having enough of this, I was about to leave when she let out a frustrated scream.

"Why don't you get it? Your wife is gone and I am beside you now. Doesn't it feel great to get rid of her and be with me instead, like how it was originally supposed to be?"

"What in the world are you talking about?" My voice lowered as she kept saying things that fueled my anger. "Thank you for rescuing me, but keep your distance, I'm a married man. It's my last warning towards you"

"Then...I'll be happy to be your concubine. Won't you accept it seeing how I'm even satisfied with this rank?" She sounded like a mad woman trying to desperately hold on, something I would never expect from her.

"Forgive me but I don't want anyone other than Goeun. You see..We made a promise to each other"

She gritted her teeth before tears started to well up in her eyes. "Do you know how much I tried to get rid of that woman? I thought you would come back to me if she disappeared. Like come on, she's just a weak little girl who doesn't even have anything you like."

"Do not speak of my wife in that manner. I swear to god Minah, I will throw away our years of knowing one another right this instant, and it's not going to be pretty"

Laughing bitterly, she sat down before saying "too bad, I told your wife that once I save you, I deserve to be by your side. That naive girl, she actually left once we came back, even worrying about my injuries."

The truth was finally out and she looked up at me even more frightened realizing her slip up. Something seemed to switch in me as I pushed her to the wall, landing a punch to the spot beside her in anger. "You're making me regret every moment of me ever liking and waiting for you. I- I truly wasted my life on you"

"Your mother would disagree. She loved me and wanted me to always stay by her son's side" Seeing how she was using my mother as her last resort, I realized how much she has changed for the worse.

"My mother would have adored my wife with all her heart if she was here"

Letting go, I left the room, not wanting to see her face anymore. My only goal right now was to find my Goeun, and the only person who would know the answer would be Yul and her highness.

Walking into their room, I was met with a shocked Yul who stood up in a rush to hug me tightly, not wanting to let go. "You woke up sleeping beauty. I was almost worried that something was seriously wrong with you"

Patting his back, I went straight to the point "my wife.. where is she?"

His face darkened as he let go and began to pace around the room. "I don't know, Yohan. One day she was here and the other she disappeared completely. We can't seem to find her anywhere. Hyerin has been worried sick about her whereabouts."

Running my hand through my hair, I winced in pain now noticing my bleeding knuckles. "How in the heck did you get hurt so fast?!" Yul dragged me over to the room where the royal Physician was at and I had a full checkup done on me.

"Lady Goeun really did apply the salve day and night for you determinedly. She even asked for the best medicine that could heal you faster." I looked at my body once more and saw how the bruises were much more tolerable and better than before.

"You should really take care of her now, she lost a lot of weight in a short amount of time and we barely managed to get her to eat a little better. I didn't know a person could store so much tears like that up until I met her" shaking his head, he bandaged my hands before patting my shoulder.

"Be happy now, the both of you." My heart seemed to have broken into pieces hearing snippets about my wife from the others. I miss you like crazy goeun.

I met with my own soldiers as they all came running up to me before bowing their heads. Some had their leg bandaged while some had their arms covered up. "It must've been hard fighting alone, forgive me for leaving you in that situation."

They started a commotion shaking their heads and talking over one another "it wasn't your fault General, you got hurt way worse than us." "It's okay we are healing very well thanks to my lady and the royal medic"

"My lady?" Raising my eyebrow, I waited for him to continue. "Lady Goeun was the first to take care of us and bandaged us up the day we got hurt. She really is fit to be the generals wife"

Agreeing with them, my mind drifted off to her again, wondering where she could be right now. There's so many people that know how worthy you are. Why...why do you not see that in yourself?

Part 37

About a week and a half passed by as I tried hard to find someone who was going back to the palace areas. Staying at an inn for a while really tired me out as I constantly had to be on the move. Will I have to be stuck here for the rest of my life?!

I have to go back before Yohan and the rest start their journey, so I can pack up my stuff in our house. Although I thought that I was managing better than expected when I left, it was proven false when I woke up one day in the infirmary. The owner of the inn couldn't wake me up so she had someone carry me to get checked out.

Thankful for her service, I paid her double and then stayed for treatment. Am I lovesick or something? Chuckling at my horrible sense of humor, I took off the braids in my hair that were causing me to have a headache. Letting my hair flow down, I laid in bed, not knowing what to do with my life anymore.

Grabbing the small bag of mine, I pulled out his shirt before snuggling into it, easing my pain for a bit, forgetting about the world around me. I regretted my decision a lot after that day, thinking of the what ifs. What if Yohan is searching for me? What if I'm not as replaceable as I thought I was?

Shaking off the thoughts, I got up before paying for my stay. Going out into the streets again, I walked a bit on the side, not wanting to attract any attention. However, I was still alert, trying to find any carts or carriages I can ask for a ride in. I'll never be able to go back alone because I am confident that I will get lost in the first hour.

Once I turned the corner to a small alley, my body got pushed against the wall, the person's hands protecting my back and head from the impact. Closing my eyes shut I tried to get away from them, scared of what they want to do with me.

"Put your hair up this instant"

My eyes snapped open at the familiar voice as I looked at his face for confirmation. There stood the man that I had been wanting to see badly for weeks now, alive and well. Scanning his body, once I checked that he was alright, I sighed in relief.

"Did you not hear me?" Finally processing his words, I touched my hair realizing that I never bothered to put it back up again. "Why are you here?" Pushing him away gently, I could sense the hurt in his eyes as he pulled me even more closer to him.

Gasping in surprise, I shook my head before trying to move away from him, when my heart was screaming for me to do the opposite. "Why are you leaving me? You promised that you wouldn't ignore me" His eyes held so much yearning that I almost gave in to him, until I remembered what I had told Minah.

"No..I can't do this. I told her that she"

"Don't even think of finishing that sentence. Did you ever think of how I would feel once I woke up and saw that my wife left me saying another woman is good for me? What kind of bullshit is that?!"

I kept my eyes on the ground not knowing what to say until he lifted up my chin "look at me, Goeun. Please look at me while I'm speaking" Gaining the courage to look at him in the eye again, I finally spoke up in a calm manner.

"She kept harassing me Yohan, I didn't know what to do when she continued with her insults. She truly made me believe that you deserve someone that can protect you, especially during times like those" looking over at his head, I reminisced the blood that was all over his head.

"No, I want someone like you, even if I don't deserve it. I only want you, I want- no need Kim Goeun in my life" Taking my hand, he gently kissed it before putting it on his cheek, as if feeling the warmth of it.

My face flushed at the amount of affection he was displaying, making it harder and harder to pull away. "Yohan, you should've seen yourself when she brought you back. You were both in a bad condition but without her, we wouldn't have been able to save you-"

"I love you" his words left me speechless as I struggled to form the next thing to say. "Wait that's not fair" pouting, I looked at him with a frown, leaving him confused.

"What's with that reaction? I thought you would jump on me by now" I almost got annoyed by how spot on he was because I really thought of doing that. "You can't just say those words so easily, it makes it harder for me to reply to that" As I tried to think of what else to say, Yohan suddenly guided my hands to his neck before flashing me one of his captivating smiles.

"It's actually easy baby, all you have to say is I love you back. I'll do the rest" My heart raced at his flirty attitude before finally giving in to him.

"...I love you too" although I rushed out those words, he understood me perfectly, before crashing his lips onto mine, his mouth eager to explore, biting my lower lip and asking for entrance. He then moved on to kissing my earlobe and collarbone before going down to my neck. Placing many soft kisses, he spent extra time sucking on the area that made my toes curl due to the sensation.

Circling his thumb over my shoulder, he kept still for a while, as we stared at each other silently. "Come home with me" speaking softly, he waited for my response with anxious eyes.

"And if I don't?" Raising my eyebrows, I only meant to joke around with him but he literally picked me up in the way people carry their sack of potatoes. "I'll just have to kidnap you then"

"Wait are you crazy?! Aren't you hurt everywhere? I'll walk on my own, put me down" slapping his back lightly, I thought he would finally listen to what I said but he put me down before picking me up again. That repeated for a bit as I stared at him with a "are you kidding me" look.

"That, is to prove that I'm in good shape again. And secondly, it's to see how much weight you lost from the last time I saw you."

"I guess we both lost weight, but you look like you haven't been sleeping" Sliding my finger over his dark circles, I could tell how tired he looked.

"My hugging pillow disappeared one day so I couldn't sleep without it." Smiling at that, I turned somber realizing exactly what I had just done. "I can't just shamelessly run back to you and pretend that nothing happened. I have to take responsibility for my words and actions."

"Yul, Her highness, my men, the royal doctor, and especially me. We are all waiting for you to return with open arms. So you shouldn't hesitate anymore." All this time, I've been considering myself as someone who could be forgotten, as everyone else will continue on with their lives. An unimportant piece in a board game that is neither valuable or useful.

But seeing him look at me like this and hearing that so many people are waiting for me, made me finally realize. That I'm a person worthy of love, that there's others who care about my wellbeing.

...Goeun is someone significant..

Part 38

"What..are you doing?" Feeling my hair being pulled up by Yohan as we were walking, he didn't seem to let go which got me confused.

"They're staring at you right now" Looking over at him, I saw how he was glaring at the men passing by, making me burst into laughter. "They're probably staring because of the little stunt you're doing with my hair" With a huff, his glaring never stopped as he let go of my hair before placing his hand around my waist. Hmm, I love seeing him jealous

I, too, then covered his face with my arm, leaving him puzzled with my actions. "All those women are staring at you as well, so I can't help but cover your face for the rest of the time here.""Or should I get a face veil made especially for you?" Swatting my arm away, he had on an amused expression, his smile contagious.

"Okay enough joking around, we have to discuss something important." As he led me inside one of the shops, the thought of a possible war made me halt in my steps. "What happened with the neighboring enemies? Are you planning to go into battle again?"

"Yul said he and his majesty will try to handle it themselves for now. If fighting is needed, then I'll-"

"I see"

Cutting him off, I had a hard time keeping my heart steady as my mouth dried up from anxiety. Flashbacks of the soldiers hurt on the ground, their cries of pain, the stench of blood in the air, and especially my husband lying down still as if he were dead came to mind. I couldn't shake off the feeling that this might happen again, and so soon. Closing my eyes, I tried to calm down as I suddenly felt out of breath. My ears felt blocked as if I was underwater, the sound of only muffled voices was heard.

1...

"..."

2...

"..eun"

3...

"What's wrong? Do you want to rest for a bit?" I came back to reality once I saw Yohan looking down at me with concern. Trying to hide my trembling hands, I let out a smile before shaking my head.

"Okay then, but when I said we needed to talk about something important, it wasn't about that." Sitting down, I finally noticed that we came here to eat, looking at the tables next to us. "A bowl of stew and seaweed soup"

The lady working here got us our meals and rice on the side. "It must be your birthday today! You precious little thing, you have to thank your mom for giving birth to you. Childbirth isn't an easy thing" Patting my back a few times, she left to continue on with her work.

"Although I'm about two weeks late, happy birthday Goeun"

Tucking my hair behind my ear, I waited for him to start eating before putting the rice in the soup. Taking a big bite, I nodded my head in approval of the taste.

"So this is what you wanted to talk about?" He looked rather pleased with himself and this situation, making me smile unknowingly.

I can't with him..

"You idiot, how dare you leave me? If you had told me, I would've gone with you" Hyerin has basically been attached to me ever since I came back to the residence, not letting me out of her sight.

Just in time, Prince Yul dragged her away, pulling her to his side protectively. "I don't think that's a very good idea. Do you want the whole nation looking for you?" As they were busy bickering with one another, I watched them with a smile on my face. Yohan told me that Hyerin was devastated after she heard about the whole story of Minah and us. She was mad that no one told her earlier, especially at her husband.

When we were eating a while ago, Yohan literally said "I don't know if he's even alive right now". Minah left to the palace earlier than the rest of us, which was probably done by the orders of his highness. Although I do feel bad about it, I also realized I should learn to not feel guilty for being happy on my own. I know it's selfish of me, but I'm tired of trying to take responsibility for things that aren't in my control.

Going back inside my room, I noticed Yohan's back on me as he was taking off the bandage around his chest. Walking over to him, I examined his body which had a few bruising still visible. "Do you want me to apply the salve for you?"

Before I could smear some on, he took hold of my wrist before arching his brow. "Where did the innocent Goeun go? You used to blush just by looking at me shirtless"

"I don't get flustered over those things anymore" Flipping my hair back, I applied it onto him with a confident smile, until he sneakily guided my hand elsewhere.

"How about now?" With a mischievous glint, he leaned closer to me, making me turn into a red tomato. "I'd like to take back my words now" Pushing him away, I ran to escape to the door as he chased after me laughing.

"Come back here"

Waking up from a nightmare isn't the best feeling, as I got up to grab his shirt instinctively. But upon realizing where I was and the person sleeping next to me, I got back in the covers.

Grabbing his hand for comfort, I tried to calm down without disturbing him. It was the same dream again, where I saw everyone dead on the ground, laying still in a pool of blood. Their eyes were open but at the same time empty, with no trace of life or emotion in them.

Shuffling next to me, Yohan took me in his embrace. "Your heartbeat is fast" His voice sounded a bit more raspy as he rubbed my back soothingly. It was quiet for a moment as I contemplated on whether telling him or not.

"Yohan? Can someone ever get over a traumatic experience?"

"They first learn to cope, and then build up the courage overtime to recover from it. But, it's never forgotten, as it comes back to you from time to time." Hearing that made me feel a little better, knowing that I will one day, get past it.

"How do you cope with constant blood shed and fighting?"

"I-get stronger, to not let anyone down. So that I will succeed and not suffer anymore losses"

The sound of the wind outside was heard as I processed his words carefully. I focused more on how his words was not any losses but instead anymore losses. "That's-such a huge burden for one person. But I know you'd never change that" Tightening my hold on him, I stifled a cry, not wanting to show him that I'm afraid.

"I'm always apologetic towards you, but is it too selfish of me to ask you to continue staying by my side?"

"You were so determined to take me home earlier, you even talked about kidnapping so seriously." Grinning, he shook his head no before saying "You know I would never do that to you."

"...""I think you would"

Nudging me away, he sulked as I laughed softly, trying to hug him again. We both went back to sleep with my mind a bit more at peace, thanks to the conversation we had tonight. I'll be strong too, to get over this and stay by your side confidently.

Part 39

Tomorrow was our last day here before we went back home and I suggested that we strolled around town. Who knows when I'll be able to travel again

It was going by peacefully until I noticed a familiar person walking ahead of us with a baby in his hands. They were wearing commoners clothes and a cloth bag swung around their body. Trying to take a closer glimpse at the persons face, I sneakily tried to figure out if he was someone I knew.

"What are you doing?" Yohan eyed my movements as I pointed at that man suspiciously. "I think I know him but I need to see his face to make sure" who does that person remind me of?

"Do you want to spy on him?" He stood closer to me and I nodded my head determinedly. "Teach me the way of achieving silent footsteps dear General"

I know it's probably creepy to be stalking someone all the way to their house but I had a feeling that I needed to follow him. Once he turned the corner to his gate, I saw his face for a brief moment and I let out a gasp in surprise. Smacking Yohan's shoulder a few times, no words could come out of my mouth as Yohan mouthed a what at me.

"It's my older brother"

Before he could even attempt to stop me, I was already on my way to the door. Giving it a few knocks, Yohan stood beside me nervously as I tapped my foot impatiently. "What are you going to do to him?"

"I'm going to kill him"

"Who is it?" Coming out of his place, he opened the gates only to be met with his dear sister that he has practically abandoned. The color drained from his face as he hurried to close it but Yohan stopped him from doing so.

"You're not my older brother anymore" grabbing his hair, I pulled him out as he yelled for me to let go. "So this is where you were hiding? I thought you were traveling the many nations, what happened?"

"Goeun we can talk this out! Why are you so violent, this is so unlike you!" He attempted to grab my hair but Yohan stopped him midway. We were gaining attention from the neighbors and all the ruckus caused a young woman to come out of the same house with a baby in her hands.

"What are you doing to my husband?!" She tried to pry my hands away and I let go, stunned by the new information. She stood protectively in front of him whilst glaring at me.

I bet to the others, it looked like my brother had an affair with her and I was the old lady who caught her husband in the act. "So you abandoned us and lied about what you were doing for years?" He stood behind her guiltily and I swear I wanted to smack him again.

Fixing my appearance and wrinkled up dress, I smiled at the lady in front of me. "Can I come in? I think my brother has a lot of explaining to do" She looked over at him in realization before ushering us inside. ...."So you got married?" He eyed me and Yohan and I nodded my head yes. "You didn't even come to your one and only sister's wedding"

"How long have you been married?" I snapped back as I felt a sense of betrayal.

"We got married once I found out Dasom was with a child" scratching his neck, he sat awkwardly looking between me and his wife that was in the other room.

"He told us he was busy traveling and exploring new places. The only thing he explored was a woman's-" my whispering got clamped shut by Yohan's hands as he smiled at Older brother uncomfortably. "Nice to meet you, my name is Kim Yohan"

"Forgive me for the late greetings, I'm Han Hyunwoo."

I sat there sulking at the fact that I was kept in the dark while all these things happened in his life. Is this how Hyerin felt?

"Goeun if you're mad about the fact that I didn't come to your wedding, then I'm sorry. I didn't even know you were engaged in the first place."

"No brother, I'm disappointed that you didn't care to mention that you fell in love, got married, and had an adorable baby this whole time. I wasn't even invited to my own brother's ceremony, how upsetting is that?"

Guilt was written all over his face as he tried to explain himself. "Mother would never accept the fact that I wanted to get married to a commoner. So I had no choice but to hide it from you guys. Please don't tell our parents"

Biting the inside of my cheek, I was conflicted on what to do or what to say. Miss Dasom then came out of the room with her baby girl. "May I hold her?" Giving her to me gently, she still seemed weary of me after seeing me almost pull out brother's hair earlier. I'm sorry he deserved it..

I watched as the baby slept soundly in my arms, with her mouth a little open. My heart melted at how cute she looked, with her slightly chubby cheeks and small little hands. Finally making up my mind, I looked at brother seriously. "Come back home with us tomorrow"

"Both of you. Let's introduce Miss Dasom and your baby to Mother and Father. Sure they will be upset at first but they'll soon come to accept it. Mother favors you over me anyways so she'll forgive you, especially after knowing that she has a grandchild." ....."We will come see you again, so it would be good if you were to make up your minds by tomorrow Sir Hyunwoo" Bowing his head, we were leaving when brother stopped me. "Why was he so strong when I tried to close the door earlier?"

"Because he's a General" Smiling proudly, I left to catch up with my husband.

Part 40

With a palanquin and our 3 horses, we set off to Hyunwoo's place to pick them up. There they stood with a few bags in hand, and a playful baby by their side.

"Good Morning Lady Dasom, I'm glad you guys came to this decision." Holding the palanquin open, I waited for her to get in but she stood frozen still. "I wouldn't dare to get in, I-I'm merely a commoner."

"Trust me, I would not want to walk on foot for a week with a baby." Although she protested, I managed to put her in before getting on my horse. Brother simply stared at me before getting on himself.

As we galloped through the forest, he attempted to start a conversation. "You changed a lot sister"

"How so?"

"You used to be calculative when speaking or taking action. You're more.. expressive now, as if you found your own color."

Smiling, I also agreed with him. "When you go back home, please don't add me into the story when explaining yourself. I'll come over once I send a formal letter to give notice of my visit."

Staring back at the road, I let out a sigh, despising the fact that the ride back will be so long.

A week passed by and we finally arrived. I promised myself that I will never go on such long trips again. From a certain point, everyone dispersed on their own ways to go back to their homes where I said goodbye to my brother and his wife.

Seeing our own place made me feel so happy, Yohan even noticed the difference in my attitude. Going inside, I rushed over to meet Areum after not seeing her for a whole month.

"My Lady!" Areum brightened up at our arrival before running into my embrace. "How was your vacation?"

That question made me want to puke remembering all the things we went through. "It was....quite different compared to how I imagined it to be" Leaving it at that, I didn't want to go over the details again.

"Areum, could you send a formal letter saying that we will go to my parents' house in a few days time? I bet they are in utter chaos right now" chuckling, I could already picture mother's reaction to everything. Nodding, although curious, she silently left to carry out her job.

Night quickly approached as me and Yohan sat at the balcony drinking tea like the old couple we were. We didn't realize how much we took the peace and quiet for granted so here we were, doing nothing but relaxing.

We were both wrapped up in a blanket since it was really cold outside, but the sky view looked magnificent, too good to miss. Humming a random tune, I quietly sipped my tea as Yohan was reading a book.

Soon enough, the sound of muffled voices entered my ears, piquing my interest. Following the sound, my eyes landed on the young soldier and Areum standing next to one another closely. He was the same boy who had helped me look for Nari a while back, so it was easy to recognize him.

Putting down my cup, I leaned closer to the ledge, watching their little interaction. With a basket in her hand, she was trying to feed him something while he backed away a bit, his face clearly flustered. Smirking slightly, I let them do their own thing.

"That scene looks awfully familiar" his gaze on them as well, he stifled a laugh, glancing over at me a few times.

"Come on, you know I wasn't that clingy. In fact, I knew how to give you space when you needed it." The events of the time we didn't contact each other for three months still made me scoff in disappointment.

"I didn't realize my lady gets upset easily" My body got enveloped in his blanket as he swayed us side to side.

Leaning into his embrace, I closed my eyes in bliss, grateful for how far we have come.

"What do you think life has in store for us?" Staring up at him, I watched as his lips curved into a smile that I knew of too well. "Babies?"

Smacking his arm lightly, I followed along with his teasing. "How many would you like then?"

He held up three fingers, only to watch me as I pulled down a finger so it became two instead. "I cannot handle that many kids, I don't trust myself"

"That's why you have me" He showed me three once again and I shook my head no. "How will you take care of all of us if you go off to battles? That won't work"

Both of us stared at his finger seriously, as if someone was forcing us to make a decision right this instant. Sighing, I turned around before giving him a light kiss on his forehead. A hum of approval came from him as his grip on my waist got firmer.

"Is this kiss meant to tell me that we should start on our baby number one?" I felt myself being lifted easily as a giggle escaped my lips.

"No.. but I'll be the one to pamper you tonight" whispering in his ears softly, I started to roam my hands around his body, catching him off guard with the unexpected playful actions. Fondling with the string that keeps his shirt together, I felt as his muscles tensed up, his eyes a bit hazy in expectation.

"So you want to take the lead this time?" We kept eye contact as I felt his fingers take out the hair pin as he undid my braid carefully.

"I'll take the lead right after you take us inside. I don't think I can carry you there" wrapping my hand around his neck, I watched as he took us inside, laughing at my newfound confidence.

Tracing up from his jawline to the area behind his earlobe, I placed little kisses everywhere, using my tongue to suck and lick gently. Blowing a bit in his ear, I smiled in satisfaction as he let out a shiver in delight. "We should first set the mood... General" He swallowed his laughter as another emotion bubbled up inside both of us.

The tea on the table seemed to have been forgotten as it turned cold next to the half-open book in the corner. Oh well...those can be continued on another day

----

Many months later

"You need to push my lady! Take a deep breath and exhale before trying again!"

Grunts and cries could be heard from outside the door as I felt traumatized hearing them. We came rushing to the palace after hearing of Hyerin's labor beginning and I wanted to support her during this difficult time but it turns out I'm the one who needs reassurance.

"Her highness will be fine, Yul is in there as well. We just have to be patient" Yohan put his hand on my thigh to stop me from shaking my leg nervously.

"At this rate, I think I will be okay with only one pregnancy" mumbling to myself, I didn't realize Yohan heard me until he said "It is your body, your choice Goeun. I won't allow anyone to force you otherwise"

Smiling at that, we both waited and Yohan came up with many things to talk about to let time pass. "Do you remember what you got me for my birthday?"

"hmm, I made you a warm scarf since you lost yours and couldn't find it anywhere."

"You embroidered little hearts on the bottom.. did you think it matched my style?"

I crossed my arms before nodding my head. "I heard you wore it proudly in front of your soldiers. Doesn't that mean you liked it?" The corner of his lips turned up, and I knew he was going to say something to try to woo me again.

"I like to show off whatever my wife gives me"

"But what about that lucky charm I gave- it"

"We do not speak of that" shushing me in the process, both of our heads turned to the closed door once we heard a baby's cry echoing through the halls.

"She did it"

Prince Yul came out from the door with his hair messy and a bit sweaty. If I wasn't aware of what was going on in there, I would've assumed that he was the one who went through labor.

"Well.. he did something I guess" Yohan got up before giving his friend a hug, congratulating him. These were one of the rare times where I saw them showing affection like this, so I watched from a distance, letting them do their thing.

I waited for a while, making sure that the baby and his mother was cleaned up before I entered quietly. Hyerin still looked like her cheerful self despite the fact that she went through excruciating pain just a while ago. I wonder how mothers jump back into action right after giving birth. I would need to take a week off from everything and everyone just to gather back my energy.

"I'm so proud of you Rin-ah, how are you feeling now?" Sitting down next to her, I watched as she cradled her little one in her arms gently. He was so tiny and fragile, I don't think I would be able to hold him without panicking a little.

"It felt like my lower half was being ripped apart just a while ago but I seemed to have forgotten all the pain once I saw him for the first time. I still can't believe I'm a mother now"

"I-" before I could speak, an elegant woman with a few ladies behind her came rushing in, without even notifying us.

"Let me see my grandson, how is he? They said he's perfectly healthy right?" Realizing that this was the queen, Hyerin's mother in law, I bowed my head before quietly making my way to the door.

Looking over at Hyerin one more time, I smiled before waving a little, which she replied with a nod. I had mixed emotions to how her mother was reacting, just caring for the baby and not Hyerin herself. It seems palace life is still complicated no matter how happy we are. However, we still show our respect towards them because of their social status.

Making my way out of the palace grounds, I let out a sigh of relief, to which Yohan noticed immediately. "What's bothering you?"

"If I say the air, would you still fight it for me?"

"Of course, what you want, I will get" He somehow still comes up with better answers to my jokes, making me amazed every time.

"You better not get a concubine later on in our life."

"What's with the sudden possessiveness?" Linking my hand in his, I watched as he was grinning from ear to ear.

"I've become really greedy lately. I need to keep all this affection to myself." Walking to the palanquin, he waited for me to get in before saying "If this is what you call being greedy, then I don't mind it one bit"

Epilogue

Sitting in my old room again felt nostalgic as me, mother, and Dasom were busy sorting out clothes for her baby. I knew mother would come by and now she was the one spoiling her grand child every time they came over.

I watched how there were little sets of everything, many pairs of shoes and ribbons for her hair to choose from. As I held a light blue dress in front of me, mother let out a sigh before whispering to me and Dasom.

"Goeun, is your husband perhaps....impotent?"

I choked on literal air listening to mother's words as a blush ran up to my cheeks. "Mother! How could you say that about your son in law?"

"Its been a while since you got married and everyone around you has been having kids already. Is something wrong with him, or is it you?"

"We both agreed to wait a while before having kids..it is a big responsibility. And um.. I told him I wanted to go through only one pregnancy"

Mother slapped my arm and Dasom calmed her down to which I was grateful for.

"Then I will pray for god to bless you with twins in one pregnancy. You'll endure the pain once and be granted two beautiful children. Doesn't that fit your criteria?"

I stood speechless at mother's words but couldn't say anything smart back because it did make a little sense.

We all came out of the room for lunch where we saw the three men playing go, a board game together on the table. Brother was playing against father as Yohan silently gave some tips to father so he could win.

Pulling him aside for a bit, I whispered in his ears. "You earned yourself the reputation of an impotent man, Mother thinks you're like that" Something flashed in his eyes and just as he was about to retaliate, I ran off to Dasom's side. Sticking out my tongue, I laughed as his ears turned red and he couldn't keep eye contact with mother for a while.

The one thing that got me nervous was when he mouthed the words "wait until we go home" to which I shook my head no. He couldn't do or say anything afterwards since everyone was present in the room, which I took advantage of.

After eating lunch, we had to depart early since Yohan said he had something urgent to do at the palace. I bid my farewells to everyone and kissed my cute niece on the cheek goodbye.

After a long while, we came to a stop and I went inside the gates with the permission of being with Yohan. I had finally been granted a gate pass but hadn't brought it with me today. Before we were able to go into his room, a familiar figure came in front of us. She looked surprised at first but quickly masked her expressions to one of serious professionalism.

"Good evening, it's surprising how we meet like this"

It really was unexpected since Miss Minah had been promoted to a better position in the royal court. After his majesty found out that she was the one who led the rescue operation, he took notice of her skills and knowledge. She was now in a higher place as she travels and gets work done from outside the capital. It's rare to spot her in the palace so it has been a while since I've last seen her.

"I've had some work to do now, so I must take my leave. Good day, Lady Goeun and General Kim." We both bowed to one another before going our own separate ways. We all knew in our heads that there was now a certain line to keep with one another, so I could feel the weird atmosphere between the three of us.

Once we got inside the study room, Yohan suddenly turned around almost making me run into his chest. "So what were you saying earlier in mother's house?"......

Seeing Yohan's indifferent attitude towards Miss Minah and her respectful attitude towards him, I realized something that day. First loves are thought to be the most exciting part of our lives as they sweep you off the ground, where everything feels pure and new. You experience your firsts with them intimately, first hug, first kiss, first fight, and a first breakup. Although it is the most passionate time of your life, that doesn't mean it's the best or the deepest.

However, true love comes to you when you least expect it, that person completes you and you feel more like yourself with them. You share your joys and worries with them and they root for your dreams and goals wholeheartedly. You accept them as who they are without seeking change, and you embrace one another's insecurities. You start to see your future with them as you stare into their eyes daily. You see beauty in their imperfections and realize that "this person is someone who I will cherish for the rest of my life."

Everyone close to Yohan expected him to turn back to his first love, because in fairytales, in those sweet romance novels, that person is irreplaceable. No matter what you do, you will end up going back to them because that's the magic with first loves. But looking at my husband now, I realized a person matures as they age and their perspective on a relationship differs as well. If you ask me, Kim Yohan is my first, last, true, and best love, who appeared in my life when I needed him the most. He is my pillar of support who always believed in me, no matter what anyone said or however much they belittled me. He chose to stay by my side and I promised to do the same in return.

I, Kim Goeun, will live happily with this man, my dear General._____

www.ingramcontent.com/pod-product-compliance
Lightning Source LLC
Chambersburg PA
CBHW072155070526
44585CB00015B/1146